THE BEDOUIN

By the same author
The Egyptians: How They Live and Work

THE BEDOUIN

Shirley Kay

Crane, Russak & Company Inc. New York
David & Charles   Newton Abbot   London   Vancouver

British Library Cataloguing in Publication Data

Kay, Shirley
  This changing world, the Bedouin.
  1. Bedouins – Social life and customs
  I. Title
  956'.004'927   DS219.B4

  ISBN 0–7153–7532–6

Printed in Great Britain
by Redwood Burn Limited Trowbridge
for David & Charles (Publishers) Limited
Brunel House Newton Abbot Devon

Published in the United States of America
by Crane, Russak & Company, Inc.
347 Madison Avenue New York New York 10017

ISBN 0–8448–1228–5
Library of Congress Catalog Card Number 77–88174

Published in Canada
by Douglas David & Charles Limited
1875 Welch Street North Vancouver BC

CONTENTS

INTRODUCTION

The bedouin are nomadic Arabs who live by rearing sheep and camels in the deserts of the Middle East. They came originally from the Arabian peninsula, moving northwards in ancient times into the deserts and cultivated areas of the Fertile Crescent. In the early seventh century, they advanced across North Africa into Spain, and eastwards to Iran and Asia, carrying the banners of Islam.

In the centuries that followed the Islamic expansion, many Arab tribes trekked westwards from Arabia into the Sahara. Today they live there still, alongside the Tuareg, the original nomadic Berber inhabitants of that great desert. The Tuareg have a different cultural background from the bedouin, their men are veiled, for instance, and their women play a stronger role, but basically their way of life is the same.

The word 'bedouin' is the western version of the Arabic word *badawi-yin* which means 'inhabitants of the desert', the *badiya*. The singular in Arabic is *badawi*, but in English the one word 'bedouin' has come to be used for both singular and plural, and I have used it thus. Strictly speaking the term 'bedouin' should only be applied to the noble camel herding tribes, but again it has been used as a general term in English to cover all nomadic Arabs. The nomads usually refer to themselves as the *'arab* while the townsmen refer to them as 'the tribes'.

Names of tribes and individuals have been transliterated into English in many different ways by different writers. I have tried, for the sake of easy recognition, to keep to the most common transliteration consistent with a reasonably accurate rendering of the Arabic. The alphabet which

7

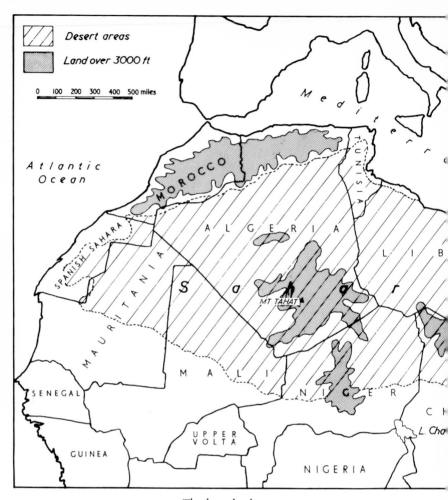

1 The desert lands

we use today was first developed in the deserts and towns of the Fertile
Crescent, some of the earliest examples of alphabetic writing coming
from the Sinai desert. However, our alphabet has now diverged con-
siderably from the Arabic and a strict transliteration requires the marking of long vowels and the use of apostrophes to denote sounds which do
not exist in English. This can be tiresome to read, especially for the reader

8

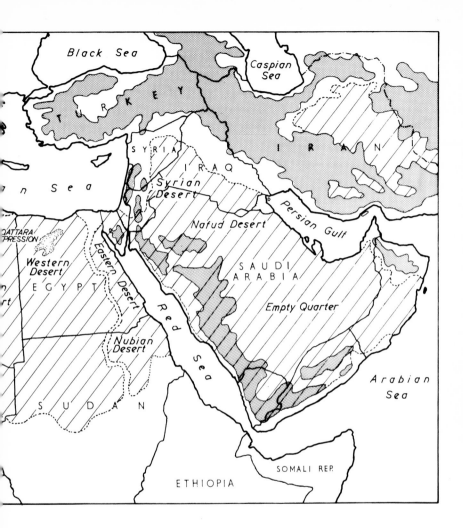

unaccustomed to such devices. I have, therefore, not in general made use of these signs. I should point out, however, that this can lead to confusion with the word 'al': when used before a tribal name, as in Al Murrah, Al Saud, it has a long 'a' and means 'family of'; in other contexts it is the Arabic word for 'the'.

Western culture and beliefs deriving from the Old Testament are

9

often descended from bedouin culture and ideas as the Old Testament is, in a large part, the story of bedouin tribes of the Fertile Crescent. The ancient Bible stories come to life if they are re-read with a picture of today's bedouin in mind. Often people describe scenes of bedouin life as 'biblical'.

The days of this bedouin culture may, however, now be numbered. The discovery of oil under the deserts has brought greater and swifter changes to the life of the Middle East than have ever been experienced by any peoples throughout history. Immense wealth is percolating through all levels of Arab society, affecting even the remotest bedouin. In the past few years they have started to use many new objects in their tents; they have adopted motor transport with enthusiasm, and they have been tempted to leave the desert to seek a better life in the towns.

Some observers judge that in a generation's time there will be no more bedouin in the deserts of the Middle East. This moment of transition is therefore an appropriate one at which to look at their life as it used to be, as it is now, and as it might become.

I

LIFE IN THE BLACK TENT

As the morning sky begins imperceptibly to lighten, at the moment when 'a white thread can be distinguished from a black one', a clear call rings out across the silent desert from the group of black tents. It is the call to morning prayer. The men emerge from the tents into the chill dawn air and kneel in the sand to pray together. The women pray in their tents, then quickly kindle a brushwood fire around which the family can warm themselves. A column of smoke rises from each tent as the bedouin start their day with a glass of sweet tea, drunk without milk.

Had the call of religion not woken the tent dwellers, there is little chance they would have overslept. As dawn breaks, the animals around the camp waken and shuffle about. Sheep and goats bleat and cocks crow and the wild birds, where there are any, break into a dawn chorus. The black tent barely separates its inhabitants from the environment around them.

The tent is, however, superbly adapted to the needs of the bedouin. With its side sections closed all round, it provides shelter from the wind and warmth on winter nights. With the sides and back panels rolled up, it offers shade from the sun at midday and the benefit of any cooling breezes. It is waterproof because the hair and wool from which it is made expand when wet, and it can be easily repaired when worn by the addition of a new strip of cloth. Most important of all, the tent and its contents can be packed up and moved in only an hour or two's work.

This long, low black tent has for thousands of years been the home of the nomadic bedouin stock herders of the deserts of the Middle East.

Within its shelter they have created for themselves a relatively comfortable and happy life; a life which many of them are unwilling to renounce despite opportunities of greater luxury in the towns and the rapid developments among the settled populations around them.

To step into a bedouin tent is like stepping into a cosy human refuge in a wilderness of desolation. Outside is empty space, threatening because of its extreme aridity and the great heat which beats down for most of the day. Inside is a tidy, well ordered home. Ornate, internal, woven wall sections, called *qata*, divide the tent into a number of living quarters; folded quilts, rugs and blankets are piled against these dividing walls. At the back of the tent are sacks of grain, leather bags full of water, dates, coffee beans or yogurt, and perhaps a brightly coloured, enamelled tin trunk in which clothes are kept. Hanging from the tent pole there might be a leather cradle for a baby. There are often a few exotic objects as well – a radio, a sewing machine, a cold box and a paraffin lamp.

One section of the tent is reserved for the men and their guests. A coffee hearth is scooped in the sand in front of this section, and a line of coffee pots, a pestle and mortar and a roasting pan stand ready to hand. Rugs are spread out on the ground, and there are cushions or camel saddles on which the men may lean. The women do not usually go into this part of the tent, but, if a woman's husband is away, she may act as host and receive unexpected guests there herself.

More commonly the women watch their husbands talking to the men of the camp or their guests by peeping over the dividing wall from their own quarters. The women's part of the tent is where the family lives and sleeps, and where their food is cooked. If several nuclear families are living in one tent, the living area may be divided by piles of stores and bedding, or by further dividing walls, to give each group a section of their own.

Around the front of the tent a rough hedge of brushwood may be built, to give the family shelter from the wind and greater privacy, and to provide a ready source of firewood. Some yards away another tent will stand, and then another and another. The bedouin camp in family groups ranging from two or three to twenty or thirty tents; they pitch

2 A typical bedouin camp in Arabia today. The family own both traditional black tents and modern square white tents bought in the local town. The striped rear section of the black tent is shown (*author*)

camp together and then move on together a week or so later, or whenever the grazing for their animals demands it.

The tent is owned by the senior woman of the family, and has probably been made by her as well. The women weave long strips of goat-hair cloth, or mixtures of goat, sheep and camel hair; they then sew these strips together to form the tent. The strips are some 60–70cm wide (2–2¼ft) their length ranging from 11 to 45m (12–49yd), depending on the required size of the tent. These strips may be bought from other bedouin, or from markets in the towns, and today white cotton sections are often incorporated in the tent as well, or a square, white, machine-made tent may be bought in town and set up beside the black one.

The tent cloth is supported by a line of central poles. There are usually two or three of these, but a wealthy shaikh may have four or even five, while a poor family may have just one. In the Sahara single-pole tents are the most common, the tent cloth being woven with coloured stripes

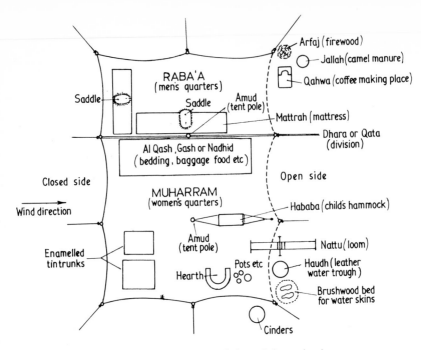

Arfaj (firewood)
Jallah (camel manure)
Qahwa (coffee making place)
Mattrah (mattress)
Dhara or Qata (division)

RABA'A (mens quarters)
Saddle
Amud (tent pole)
Saddle

Al Qash, Gash or Nadhid (bedding, baggage food etc)

Closed side

Open side

Wind direction

MUHARRAM (women's quarters)

Hababa (child's hammock)

Amud (tent pole)

Nattu (loom)

Enamelled tin trunks

Pots etc
Hearth

Haudh (leather water trough)

Brushwood bed for water skins

Cinders

3 The interior of a two-poled tent (*after Dickson*)

which often denote the owner's tribe. In Arabia only the back wall is striped and the stripes are white. The front, back and sides of the tent are supported on lower, subsidiary poles, giving an oblong shape rising to its highest point along the central ridge. Other than at this central point, the tent roof is never very high, and tent dwellers tend to sit rather than stand in their homes.

Clothing

All bedouin wear loose flowing clothes in which it is easy to sit comfortably on the floor. Unlike Europeans, who rush to strip off their clothes at the first sign of sunshine, the bedouin are always totally covered from head to foot. They have learnt through generations of experience that the safest way to withstand the fierce sunshine of the desert is to protect every inch of their persons. Only their hands and feet and a small part of

14

their faces are exposed. They rarely take off their clothes nor do they wash them very often, because of the lack of water. And as a result of living so close to their animals, they are plagued by lice, fleas and swarms of flies.

The men and boys wear a long cotton gown cut straight like a long shirt, white, grey or brown in colour. On their heads they wear a small white cap covered by a loose head cloth, white, red and white, or black and white, called a *keffiyeh* or *gutra*. This is held in place by a double black cord known as the *'agal*. On formal occasions, or when the weather is cold, the men wear a long cloak of fine wool, cream, brown or black in colour and edged with gold thread; in really cold weather they wear a European-style jacket or a sheepskin coat.

Women and girls wear long dresses with long sleeves, and beneath them long cotton pants reaching to the ankles, and perhaps another long dress as well. In the past the women wore traditional dark-blue dresses. Today ethnic hand-embroidered dresses are still made and worn by bedouin women in Palestine and Syria. In Arabia they make or buy dresses in brilliant colours from the synthetic fabrics available in the

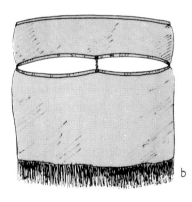

a   b

4 Face masks worn by bedouin women: a) is from the eastern region of Arabia and the Gulf states. It is made of calico dyed with indigo and has a stiff ridge running vertically along the nose, giving the woman a hawk-like appearance; b) a mask from central Arabia made of soft black material and worn longer or shorter according to taste

towns, or wear the traditional dress of the settled folk of the region in which they happen to be.

The women cover their heads with a piece of black cloth. Some cover their faces as well, while others are unveiled. This custom varies from tribe to tribe, and the veils often reflect those worn by the settled people of the region. In the north of the peninsula the women are generally unveiled. The Al Murrah of south-east Arabia wear the indigo-dyed, calico face mask of the eastern region; in central and west Arabia many bedouin women wear a black material veil with eye slots; some, in the western coastal region, wear a thick material mask, decorated with coins and buttons like the village people. Within a camp one woman may be veiled and another unveiled. Whether veiled or not, they usually use black kohl as eye make-up, to great effect and many women, especially the older ones, have their faces decorated with blue tattoo marks and make similar patterns on their hands with henna.

Both men and women wear their hair long. In the past the men plaited their hair down the side of the face; today they have abandoned this custom, but their shoulder-length hair still differentiates them from the

5 (*Opposite*) A bedouin mother wearing traditional jewellery and with tattoos on her face (*Popperfoto*)

6 (*below*) A Sulubba wedding in Syria in the early 1940s. The bridegroom has his hair plaited in a style which was characteristic of bedouin men until recent times (*Photo Giraud*)

townspeople who disapprove of long hair. The women often have waist-length hair which they may treat with henna.

Food

Under their clothes the bedouin wear a belt of plaited leather thongs and it is said that they can reduce the pangs of hunger by tightening this. They all know hunger in their lives, and most are as thin and light-built as birds. A pædiatrician who treats bedouin children today has remarked that all are more or less undernourished. Food has always been, and still is, scarce in the desert, though the advent of motor transport and tinned foods has brought some improvement.

Milk and milk products from their flocks and herds form the mainstay of the bedouin's diet. Milk is drunk warm straight after milking, or is made into yogurt by being heated and left to stand with a little of yesterday's yogurt, or shaken in a goat skin hung from a tripod. It is usually drunk as a semi-thick liquid. Many bedouin meals consist solely of a bowl of milk or yogurt.

The main meal of the day is eaten in the evening. It is cooked over an open fire in a large tinned copper pot. The family sit around the communal meal which is served on a large round aluminium platter with raised edges. They curl one leg underneath them and sit with the other knee raised in front of them, on which to rest their arm. All eat with the right hand only. The meal consists usually of rice flavoured with a little clarified butter called *ghee*. Nowadays tinned tomato paste or tinned fish add welcome variety. The meal may end with a handful of dates.

Sometimes the women make round unleavened loaves of bread. They grind the grain in a stone quern, knead it with a little water, and then throw it from hand to hand until it becomes round and thin like a pancake. Very thin loaves are baked on a convex metal baking dish; smaller thicker ones are buried in the embers of the fire until cooked.

This monotonous diet is rarely relieved by any other fare. Meat is a luxury eaten only a few times a year by poor bedouin, and then usually for a festival or on the arrival of a guest. Locusts are thought a great delicacy; they are cooked and eaten immediately, or roasted, ground up and stored to add flavour to future meals. The large monitor lizard is eaten by some tribes, and game such as gazelle, oryx and bustard were once much enjoyed but are now rare and protected.

Despite their poverty – the bedouin have the lowest per capita income in the lands where they live – and their lack of physical luxuries, the bedouin do not see themselves as the poor relations of settled folk. On the contrary, they are totally convinced of their superiority. Fidelity Lancaster (see bibliography where all authors mentioned in the text are listed), lived with her children in a bedouin camp for a year, and found the women talked little about child rearing: '. . . the nearest they got was the firm belief, constantly reiterated, that Bedouin ways were best, and that the desert was better than anywhere else'. Other travellers have often commented on this bedouin pride – self assurance verging on arrogance, which admits no possibility that other ways could be as good as theirs – Donald Cole noted that the bedouin rejected the city as physically and socially polluted; to them only the desert life was pure and clean.

The bedouin, as a result, live in their deserts not as poor gipsies or tramps, but as an impoverished nobility. Their life is organised according to a strict set of rules; to break these rules is considered 'shameful', the worst criticism that can be levelled at a bedouin. To abide by them, even to excess, brings honour and glory, the greatest reward in the bedouin world. Wilfrid Thesiger tells of a poor, ragged old man being received with immense respect by his bedouin companions. Why, he asked them later, did they spend so much care and attention on such a ragged fellow. He was the most generous man in the desert, they replied, a man who had once been very rich and had given everything away in gifts and lavish hospitality.

Hospitality

Hospitality is a cardinal rule in the desert, and one on which many lives must have depended over the centuries. All bedouin comply with the strict code of hospitality – a stranger may go up to any tent and be sure that he will be received there, even if he is from an enemy tribe. His hosts must extend to him three days' board and lodging, and protect him

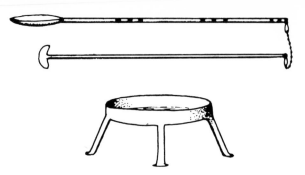

7 A metal pan for roasting coffee beans, and the stirring implement which accompanies it. The handles of pan and stirrer are usually decorated with incised patterns

while he is with them. After three days he must be allowed to leave in peace.

One evening I was sitting with my children in the tent of some bedouin whom I did not know, in southern Jordan. As it began to grow dark I felt anxious and said I must leave. My hosts pressed me to stay, so to excuse myself I explained that my elderly father was wandering about outside looking for us. 'Have no fear for him,' they replied confidently, 'there is no one here but bedouin.'

When a guest arrives at a bedouin tent a rug is immediately spread for him on the ground, and he will probably first be served with very sweet tea in small glasses brought in on a brightly coloured enamelled tray. This is brewed by boiling tea, sugar and water together in a coloured enamelled tea pot. While he is drinking the tea, the main preparation of bedouin hospitality will be under way – the ritual of making coffee. A few coffee beans are taken from the leather bag in which they are kept, and are lightly roasted in a long-handled iron skillet, being stirred with a long handled implement. Skillet and stirrer both have ornately worked handles and are attractive objects, suitable for use before guests.

The beans are then poured into a decorated wooden dish to cool, before being pounded in a mortar. All of these objects are decorative and there is a talent in using them well, the rhythmic ring of the pestle in the mortar being a measure of the host's skill. A brass or copper coffee pot is filled with water which is brought to the boil over the fire, and the

8 Traditional wooden bowls used for milking, holding food, etc. Such bowls must have been prized for they were frequently repaired, sometimes several times over. Both these bowls show signs of repair which was done either with leather stitching or with metal clips. The lower bowl has brass studs decorating the lip

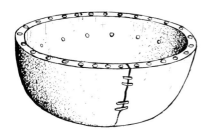

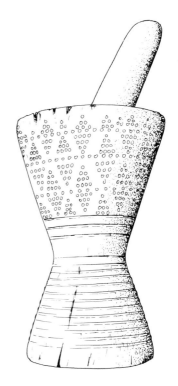

9 Wooden mortar and stone pestle used for grinding coffee beans. The mortar is decorated with white metal studs and incised bands

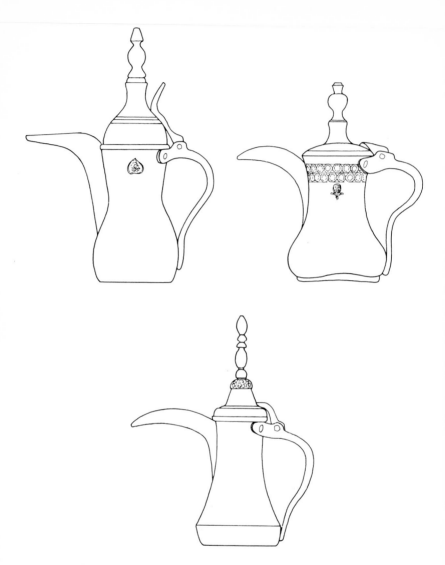

10, 11 and 12 Examples of copper and brass coffee pots which give the opportunity for a wide range of design and decoration. Several of these pots stand beside the coffee hearth in a bedouin tent and are eagerly put to use when a guest arrives or when the men gather together in the evenings ground coffee poured in. This is brought to the boil again three times, after which it is poured into a pot containing a few ground cardamom seeds.

The coffee is served to the guest in an eggcup-shaped china cup. It is unsweetened, a greenish colour, and flavoured with the cardamom. When the guest has drunk his tiny cupful, the cup is filled again and this is repeated until the guest holds out his cup, with his right hand, and shakes it between thumb and forefinger; this is the signal that he has had enough.

The utensils for making and serving tea have changed completely in bedouin camps in the past few years, the traditional copper teapots and trays giving way to enamelled steel, but those used in the preparation of coffee have not changed. The ritual of making the coffee is as important as the drink itself, and expresses the host's concern for his guest.

Bedouin will offer honoured guests a sumptuous meal, even if by doing so they seriously deplete their own flocks. It is common for a bedouin family to kill and cook a sheep for a guest, although they themselves may not have eaten meat for months.

This leisurely style of hospitality fits in well with the rather gentle pace of the bedouin day. The bedouin say that 'hurry is the devil's work' and they themselves are rarely seen rushing about; both the extreme heat in which they are working, and their own state of undernourishment, are against this. Much of their work is to sit all day long and watch their flocks and herds grazing. The men take the camels out in the morning, and men, women or children may look after the sheep and goats.

Fetching water has always been one of the heavier tasks which fell on the camp. Water was, and often still is, drawn by hand from a well, poured into large camel-skin bags, and carted home on camel back. Today some of the labour has gone from this task: bedouin often fetch their water by pick-up truck, transporting it in old oil drums in which they also now store it.

Girls and smaller children spend part of their time collecting brush-wood for the fires and carrying it home in bundles on their heads. This work, too, is now eased for families who own a pick-up and can bring the whole day's supply home in one journey.

On the women falls the heaviest work of the bedouin day. They must do the housework, tidy up the camp, cook and mind the small children. They spin and weave, a task which requires some physical strength. Above all they are responsible for moving camp, dismantling the tent, loading it onto camels, and re-erecting it at the new campsite. A tired bedouin woman camping with her new-born baby and other small children in a cave in Petra remarked sadly that the cave was very dirty but her tent was so heavy to erect.

It has often been said in the past that the bedouin would not work, so accustomed were they to their own free-and-easy life. This has been disproved over the past ten or twenty years, during which time thousands of bedouin have taken jobs in the cities, or with the oil companies, and worked as hard as anyone else. True, they used to dislike agriculture strongly, since throughout the ages they have always despised and bullied the peasant farmers and when set to work on agricultural projects often proved a disappointment. Today, however, many of them seem to be taking to cultivation, if left to themselves, to feed their growing flocks of sheep. They also now appear to be working harder than ever before at stock-herding – the number of bedouin remaining in the deserts has decreased sharply in the past two or three decades, but, in Saudi Arabia, for instance, where the majority of bedouin now live, it is estimated that the number of animals is as high as before.

Education

They are ambitious for their children and value education highly despite the difficulty in obtaining it. Public education is the field of development in which the greatest strides have been made in recent years throughout the Middle East. Nevertheless, education is still not universally available and the inaccessible bedouin are inevitably the most deprived in this respect.

Saudi Arabia is one of the countries which is experiencing the greatest changes as far as education is concerned. In 1958 there were still only twenty modern schools in the whole country, although many little boys were taught to recite, and some to read, the Koran. Most educated adults above the age of thirty were sent abroad for their schooling, usually to

Egypt. Nearly all the older bedouin are therefore illiterate: in a settled bedouin village Motoko Katakura found in 1970 that only four men over 25 could read while all the younger ones were literate. To obtain an education in the desert twenty years ago required superhuman efforts on the part of the child or his parents.

A few were sufficiently determined, however. One little boy, the son of a lesser shaikh in the north in those days, was fired with an over-whelming desire to learn. He succeeded in teaching himself to read with the help of any literate visitor who came to the camp. He acquired one little reading book with which he practised diligently. One day a goat ate his book and in a fit of black despair he killed the goat. The herds-man, equally angry, struck the boy and his father supported the herds-man in shaming his son.

The boy realised then that if he was to obtain the education for which he yearned, he would have to leave the tribe. He persuaded his father to let him go away to school. Eventually his studies took him to America where he obtained a doctorate and from whence he returned to achieve a high position in his homeland.

Another little bedouin, a girl, was also, surprisingly, given a good education at that time. Her father was excessively nomadic even for a bedouin and left his tribe to wander abroad. He made up his mind to send his three small children to boarding school in Egypt and the little girl entered an English school at the age of five. As a result she has grown up with the classic olive-skinned beauty of a bedouin girl, but with the skills and command of English of a British girl. Today, she enjoys a suc-cessful career as a broadcaster.

Nowadays the struggle for education is no longer the same. Three-quarters of a million children were in school in 1975, including two-thirds of the boys of primary age and one-third of the girls, though few of the girls were bedouin. The Five Year Plan, launched in that year, aimed almost to double the school enrolment by 1980, by which time it was hoped to have all boys and nearly half the girls of primary age in school. For semi-settled shepherd tribes living near cultivated areas, schooling may be easily acquired. Young boys go to the village schools, and older ones may go to secondary or night school in the towns. But for the camel herders in the inner desert, few schools are available. Some families now send their sons to stay with relatives near a school; in a few places, such as Wadi Rum in southern Jordan, governments have established special schools for bedouin children, or they may send teachers to travel with the tribes; but for most there is no school unless their family leaves the desert. In 1970 Donald Cole found that, of the nomadic Al Murrah tribe of about 15,000 people, only three boys were in secondary school and not many were in primary school.

The bedouin have little scope for sport either, although they do enjoy hawking and hunting. Fine well trained falcons are today very valuable, and it is often the bedouin who train them to fall on bustard or hares, and to renounce their quarry on the arrival of their master. The bedouin also often keep the fast salukis, game dogs related in build and speed to the greyhound. The saluki is the only dog which they do not regard as unclean, the only one allowed into their tents. Informal horse and camel races also provided some entertainment, but today these are usually organised by settled people, although bedouin may ride in them.

Religion

The semitic nomad tribes of the deserts of the Middle East have always been strongly religious – from them came the Jewish religion, from their descendants Christianity, and from the settled tribesmen of Mecca came Islam which is a powerful influence in bedouin life. It was immediately adopted by the desert tribes who carried their new religion across north Africa into Spain, and across Persia to central Asia, in a great wave of conquest in the seventh century.

Today many tribes in Arabia are strongly and devoutly religious, due largely to the influence of the puritanical Wahhabi revivals of the past two centuries. Other more remote tribes may take their religion more lightly; but, for all that, it is the basis of their social structure and beliefs. Islam teaches belief in one god, Allah; the duty of prayer five times a day; the obligation to give alms to the poor; to fast from sunrise to sunset for one month of the year, and to make a pilgrimage to Mecca once in a lifetime if possible. The social system based on these religious teachings involves the segregation of women; the right of men to have four wives at a time and to divorce them at will; stipulated inheritance for children, and protection of the rights of orphans and widows. The legal system is based on the principle of retributive justice.

Prayer times fit very naturally into the bedouin day. They are said communally when the group is together. The men stand in a line and the one who is to lead the prayers stands out in front. All face towards Mecca and, for a moment, they stand quite still, concentrating their thoughts. Then each leans his hands on his knees, then kneels on the sand, and finally bends forward to touch his forehead to the ground in submission to Allah. When the herdsmen are out alone in the desert they will pray in just the same way, facing Mecca and kneeling by themselves in the emptiness. The first call to prayer is just before dawn, when the camp awakens anyway; the second at noon when the day's heat is at its height and work stops; after this the bedouin sleep and when they waken in the later afternoon there is a third call to prayer, after which the herdsmen return to the tents with their flocks, reaching home just before dark, at the time of the sunset prayer. Two hours later there is the final prayer of the day, after which the bedouin families sleep.

It is in the life of the women in Islamic countries that the effects of religion are most marked. Traditionally women have been secluded, and among the settled populations may still virtually lead their entire lives between their own walls; apart from the men of their immediate family, they find company only among other women.

Bedouin women have been less affected by this seclusion than town and village women. Segregation is not possible for a nomadic tent-dwelling people, and the women's work is necessary to the survival of the community. Women look after the flocks of goats and sheep, and may spend long hours alone in the desert. Their safety is assured by a strict code of honour; but nothing prevents them from talking to a male friend.

Marriage and Childbirth

As a result, most bedouin marriages are based on love, rather than on family arrangements as they are in the settled communities. The preferred marriage for young bedouin is with the son or daughter of their father's brother. Girls share in the family inheritance as well as boys, and this is a way of ensuring that the family property remains intact. It also enables the girl to continue to live in the same camping group with whom she has grown up. Her cousin has first right to her hand, so if she wants to marry another she must obtain his permission first. In practice bedouin girls are rarely forced to marry against their wish, and bedouin marriages are often happy and endure a lifetime.

Men in Islam have the right to four wives, a practice which is disappearing rapidly today. Bedouin men have rarely ever had more than one, or at the most two, wives at once. They may easily divorce them, however, and this is quite common. Both partners usually marry again; unlike town women, the bedouin women are in constant contact with the whole community of the camp, which gives them a chance to meet and marry another man. Although women cannot divorce their partners with such ease as the men, they can and do return to their father's tent, and then ask for a divorce which is usually granted. By and large the bedouin are tolerant and will free their wife to marry another man.

A camel or sheep is slaughtered at the wedding, a custom also followed on other important occasions during a bedouin's life. The animal slaughtered is usually eaten, while the blood may be spilled at some important and significant spot.

A special tent is often set up for the newly wedded couple, or a section of the family tent may be partitioned off for them. Most young couples will live with the husband's parents, or in a tent set up beside theirs. The women of the family live closely together, as the men are often away from the tents during the day and may even leave for prolonged periods to work in the towns. Also the men tend to spend their evenings apart, drinking coffee in the company of other men.

Babies are born in the tents without medical attention. Although many births are easy and stories are told of women producing babies while on the move in their camel litters, or while tending the animals, others are less so, and both infant and maternal mortality are high. Motoko Katakura mentions a recently settled bedouin farmer who has lost three wives and two infants in childbirth.

Illness and Death

Until very recently the bedouin had no idea of the cause of their own or their children's illnesses, and no scientific way of remedying them. They believe in the 'evil eye' – a malignant spell which can cause sickness or death – against which such remedies as wearing blue beads, charms and talismans are tried.

Bedouin have many such superstitions and take careful note of omens which cross their path: two ravens are a favourable omen, a one-eyed person brings misfortune. A proverb advises: 'If you meet a one-eyed person, turn over a large stone,' to avert the evil.

Nowadays medical teams manage to visit many bedouin camps; the bedouin have learnt the value of preventive injections and queue happily for 'the needle'. They will also go to the towns to buy medicines, but will play safe by buying charms as well. Many will take their sick children to a clinic or hospital, but often only when they have already failed to cure them by their traditional method of branding the affected part of the body.

A touching story of the death of a bedouin child is told by Isaak Diqs who grew up a bedouin boy. One day when he came home from primary school he saw a crowd outside his tent. His little sister, Abla, who was four years old, was lying motionless inside, her mother beside her.

> My mother looked at me but did not say anything. Abla's face was turned towards the south. I realized she was dying, and that the people outside were waiting for her death. There was no time to send her to a doctor, and thus she suffered her pains alone with my mother. A few minutes later Abla died.

For a large number of bedouin the nearest doctor is many hundreds of miles away. They suffer from tuberculosis, malaria when they have been near the oases, trachoma, and gastro-intestinal troubles. It is the latter especially which kills their children. Small children dehydrate quickly in the desert, and the two- or three-day journey which may be needed to take them to a clinic is often more than they can survive. Adults and children have little resistance to disease since their ill balanced and impoverished diet leaves them with little strength. Virtually all of them are undernourished and fall prey to sickness when it strikes; on the other hand disease is less prevalent in the dry, clean atmosphere of the desert than in the villages and oases.

Children also suffer badly from the usual children's diseases to which they have little resistance owing to undernourishment. Measles is a major cause of infant mortality and whooping cough also accounts for many bedouin children's deaths. For adults, tuberculosis is by far the most serious problem, and a disease which causes high mortality. Bilharzia is also a scourge in some areas. Bedouin suffer from a wide range of anaemias, many of them congenital; in some areas, and especially in malarial oases, these have been bred to a high degree of frequency, approaching 40 per cent of the population, because anaemia gives immunity to malaria. Cancer, on the other hand, is rare, as is appendicitis, although fatal when it does strike. Accidents, however, take a heavy toll of bedouin life, especially since trucks have become so widespread.

The bedouin will set broken limbs quite successfully themselves, tying a piece of wood along the limb to hold it in place. The join usually holds well but is rarely completely straight or smooth. Their other attempts at medication are less successful since they rely on the use of camel dung and urine, spells and charms, and, above all, on burning.

Medical workers in remote clinics on the edge of the desert have remarked that the bedouin welcomed their clinics, called politely to express their appreciation when they were well, and collected a supply of aspirins or accepted innoculations happily. When they were ill, however, their first thought was to try their own traditional remedies. They would rarely come into the clinic until branding and other methods had failed.

Like any other citizen, the bedouin have the free use of all hospital facilities in Arabia and they do go to hospitals in the towns and cities. A sick bedouin may find himself in an old and rather primitive hospital, one where, for instance, mother and siblings accompany the sick child and sit around on his bed, undoubtedly making him feel much happier and more at home. Or he could wake up in the luxurious setting of the

King Faisal Specialist Hospital in Riyadh, one of the most modern hospitals in the world, where the carpeted wards look more like the bedrooms of a luxury hotel and the touch of a switch turns on colour television or draws the curtains.

In a hospital in Oman, a series of special wards were built for the bedouin. They were not quite tents but they were as out-of-doors as it was possible to make them, and there was space provided for the family to camp nearby and to cook food for themselves and their sick relative. In this way, the transition from the desert to hospital was eased and the patient was not isolated from his family group.

Medical facilities, like schools, are being rapidly expanded throughout the region. The present sixty-two hospitals and 215 clinics in Saudi Arabia, for instance, are to be increased by a further ninety-seven hospitals and 212 clinics. Bedouin families are being progressively introduced to medical treatment especially in the American-run military hospitals where the families, as well as the men themselves, are treated. These hospitals are considered to be so good that civilians often plead to be admitted.

Those who did not get to hospital and who die in the desert, are buried the day they die in shallow graves marked with a stone at head and foot. Children's graves are marked by a small oval of stones.

The bedouin believe that after death their sins and good deeds will be weighed by Allah. Alois Musil tells that the Rwala, for instance, are convinced that the scales will always dip in their favour. They will go to Paradise, a land of abundance and plentiful rain, somewhere below ground. There, all are young; they can marry and have children who are born ready grown. They own big herds and can raid hostile tribes which have been condemned to Hell.

Hell is somewhere near the sun, scorching hot and with little rain. The bedouin there have to work long, hard hours, and their camel-breeding meets with no success. Some say that neither the moon nor the stars ever shine in Hell.

The bedouin are buried in a shirt or a white shroud, and laid in the grave with their faces towards Mecca. Women are buried in deeper graves than men so that, should they ever rise in the grave, their breasts would still be covered by earth. If there are hyenas about, rocks may be piled over the grave. Only the closest women relatives may weep for the dead. That evening, or on the evening of the third day after, a sheep may be sacrificed. The grave will probably not be visited again.

Colonel Dickson tells an Awazim story of a man travelling in the desert with his young wife who was about to give birth. A baby boy was born in a rocky valley, but the mother died. Since the father had no way of keeping his new-born son alive he sadly placed his wife's body in a cave, with the baby lying on her arm, its mouth to her left breast, and walled up the entrance.

Nine months later some passing bedouin saw little footprints outside the cave. They looked through the small opening in the rough wall and saw a live boy child beside the mummified body of a woman. However the mummy's left breast and arm appeared to be still alive and the bedouin fled in terror.

The father heard the story and returned quickly to the spot. Joyfully he took his son away with him, having first buried his wife in a decent grave.

2

THE DESERT ENVIRONMENT

The nights are cold in the desert and the nomads will lie half awake and shivering in the dead hours just before dawn. It is a relief when the night begins to lighten imperceptibly towards the east and gradually a touch of blue and then of pink stains the sky. The black and white desert landscape slowly acquires a faint colour too, but it is still painted largely in shades of grey when the rim of the sun appears over the horizon. Then, rapidly, the huge bright orange globe rises, it seems, straight out of the ground; its welcome warmth is soon felt and for a few hours the desert takes on the deep colours of glowing life.

Colour is the most noticeable feature of the desert. Not the deep green splashed with golden corn or red poppies of more temperate zones; desert colour is more subtle, and constantly changing throughout the day. For a short while after dawn and before sunset, the colours are deep and vibrant: red sand dunes and cliff faces, deep orange-yellow drifts of sand, purple mountains and black basalt lava flows. As the sun climbs higher the colours are burnt out of a haze of white light, the desert becomes beige, yellow-white or grey-white, and the glare is so strong that it hurts the eyes of those unused to it. At night, by contrast, it could be a scene in a black and white photograph.

The total silence also impinges on the visitor, lying heavy on the ears – for once one is aware of 'hearing' silence. The experience is almost awesome to those used to the constant clamour of the city, as is the impression of absolute solitude. Often one can stand in the desert, look to the horizon all around and see no living thing. An occasional aeroplane passing very high overhead seems an incongruous intrusion, like a visitor from outer space.

The desert landscape is varied like its colour schemes, but everywhere the ground is barren, stripped bare by the fierceness of the sun and the lack of rain. The bedouin may live in high, wild mountains, as in the Hejaz; or among the sand dunes of the Empty Quarter, the Nefud or the Ergs of the Sahara; or, most commonly, they may live on open stony plains. The colour, shape and texture of the desert are laid bare as in a geological model. Where there are mountains one can see the structure of the rocks, the different layers and the varying composition. In western Arabia, where volcanoes were active in ancient times, the lava flows stand on the surface of the sand or rock as though they had poured out only last week. These lava flows are arid, rough and inhospitable, but they provide a safe refuge for man and beast.

Another safe refuge, because of the extreme aridity, is the area of sand dunes. Here the sand is scooped up in giant waves by the prevailing wind, and its surface is a mass of little ripples, like the surface of a lake. In extensive sandy areas the dunes may reach 300 metres (330yd) high, as they do in the Empty Quarter. A thin covering of plants can grow only in the valleys between them.

All bedouin believe the desert to be inhibited by jinns (spirits). The Al Murrah of the Empty Quarter are particularly aware of jinns in the silent emptiness of their great sand dunes. They believe the noise of the singing sands (a strange sound made by the sand dunes as the grains of sand slip down) is the work of jinns. Sometimes individual members of the tribe come out of the great desert mad, singing and laughing in a strange way. This is the work of jinns, or so the people say.

The grey stone plains provide the most hospitable terrain in the desert; the surface is hard and it is easy to travel across it. Where there is a little water, in *wadis* (valleys), or low lying areas, these plains may support a welcome growth of plants. They are bleak for lack of shelter and, in their dryer stretches, without a blade of green. But where there may be only a few plants the nomads camp.

The bedouin may cross regions where virtually nothing is growing, or may linger where the ground is covered with a thin green haze of desert shrubs brought to life by a winter rainfall. They will look for places where an irregular scatter of desert acacias provides welcome shade for man and beast and grazing for camels despite their thorns. These flat-topped trees are invariably trimmed level from below as well, at the height to which a camel's neck will reach.

The wind is a scourge in this bleak environment, for there is no natural shelter to act as a windbreak. It comes laden with fine grains of sand which sandblast the softer rocks and cliff faces, sculpting them into extraordinary shapes. At the ancient, ruined desert town of Palmyra, in northern Syria, rows of Roman columns look as though they have been gnawed by rock-eating rats about a yard above ground level. In fact that is the height at which the wind carries its heaviest sand load: they have been literally sandpapered away over the centuries.

Both men and animals suffer from this driving sand which dries and chaps the lips, blocks the nose and grates on the teeth. In bad winds, the camels are couched in a circle, heads to the centre, while their riders crouch between them. The bedouin cover the lower part of their faces with their headcloths, both to keep out the sand and to preserve a little moisture around the nose and mouth. This practical need is thought to be the origin of the Saharan Tuaregs' famous blue veils. A foreigner in the desert finds a constant need for lip-salve, a remedy not available to the bedouin. The camel, on the contrary, has developed natural protection in its long thick eyelashes and flattened nostrils.

Extremes of heat and cold are felt more sharply in a land which offers no natural protection. Although cold is not often associated with deserts, it can cause real misery and suffering. In the severe winter of 1945–6 the nomads of Algeria were estimated to have lost half their animals, the greatest losses being of sheep, 71 per cent of which perished. The bedouin's thin cotton gowns are no protection against night temperatures which may drop below freezing, and the ragged tents which are the homes of many of them offer poor insulation. In northern Arabia the more well-to-do may own a sheepskin coat, but here they may also have to cope with snow and ice.

Isaak Diqs tells of a winter when his clan were camped in ragged tents in the mountains near Hebron, after they had had to leave the warm *wadi* which had been their home. Being bedouin and independent, they did not want to join the other Palestinians in refugee camps, but the winter cold proved too much for them. 'The animals we had were killed by the cold weather and by snow', he writes. 'I still remember how those poor sheep and cows died in dozens while their owners stood looking at them, being unable to do anything for them.' When spring came the clan was left with almost no animals. They had to choose between going still further away from their homeland, or settling in a village, and the group split up. Diqs' father, alone, chose the latter course, for the sake of his sons' education.

However, extreme heat is a more common cause of suffering for desert dwellers. In summer the temperature may rise to around 55°C (130°F) in the shade, and any activity becomes agonising in the furnace-like atmosphere. The heat reverberates off the bare ground and neighbouring rocks; people dehydrate rapidly and become very thirsty for water is not readily available; they feel faint. There is a longing simply to lie down in the shade. The side and back walls of the tents are rolled up or removed, so that any passing breeze may blow through to bring a little relief. From mid-morning until mid-afternoon, while the heat is at its most relentless, the bedouin families sit or lie in the small patch of shade produced by their tent roof; the herders away from the tents seek a little natural shade where they may crouch during these worst hours of the day.

Charles Doughty, who lived with the bedouin of Arabia some 100 years ago, tells of a starving camp in summer. The animals had ceased to give milk and other supplies were all but exhausted:

> Almost as the birds must the poor Beduins live at such times of the year, when the milk is up, until the new dates. As the sun's vast flaming eye rose each day upon us with new bringing of suffocating hours, the remembrance revives in our fainting breasts of our want, with the hollow thought 'What shall be for this day's life'— and the summer I passed thus fasting and Beduin-wise, lying upon the elbow.

Until recent years, when the deserts were mapped and asphalt roads laid across them, the only means for a traveller to find his way was to trust himself to bedouin guides. The bedouin had no compass and no charts to guide them. They found their way by means of acute observation of geographical details, of a long memory, and careful study of the stars. Many bedouin travel very great distances across the peninsula with their herds, or (in the past) in the course of raids and wars, and they make it their business to learn by heart, as it were, the routes of their wanderings.

A dramatic story is told of this bedouin skill in the history of the Arab conquests. In the early days of the Islamic expansion, an Arab commander was invading Syria. He was obliged to take a route through waterless desert, to avoid the enemy fortifications. After five days without water his army were at the end of their resistance. They pressed their guide of the Tayyi' tribe to find some succour for them. He asked them to look around for a little bush, as his eyes were half blinded by the sun. They found it, dug near the roots and water trickled out. 'Praise be to God,' said the guide, 'that I have found it, for I only came this way once, as a boy.'

The nomads are not only skilled guides, they also excel as trackers. They can follow the footprints of man or beast across the deserts, and recognise the characteristics, sometimes even the identity, of the man or animals they are tracking. Donald Powell Cole, talking of the Al Murrah who live in the sands of the Empty Quarter and are famous for this ability, says that any child can recognise the tracks of all the animals that live in their desert, a teenager can tell how long ago the tracks were made and whether the creature was male or female, young or old, etc., and adults can often actually identify the man or beast. They have frequently been employed by the police to track down lawbreakers.

For night journeys, made more frequently in the past in conjuction with raiding or warfare, the bedouin had to rely on their skill in identifying the stars. The night sky is peculiarly bright in the clear air above the desert and, with so little to distract him on the ground, man naturally turns his eyes towards the stars. The bedouin can keep a direct course with the stars to guide them, and it is no chance that astronomy was one

13 It is customary for the man to ride while the woman walks. Note the woven saddle bags and the woman's veil (*Barnaby's*)

of the sciences to which the Arabs made the greatest contribution during their intellectual renaissance in the Middle Ages.

Water is the key to life in the desert, and survival depends on finding adequate supplies. Deserts are defined as areas having less than 25cm (10in) of rainfall a year, but those where the bedouin live are among the hottest and driest in the world and the average rainfall is well below this. In northern Arabia, for instance, a relatively fertile region by Arabian standards where nearly half the bedouin of Saudi Arabia live (an estimated 263,000 out of 635,000), the average rainfall is 10cm (4in) a year. In the sand wastes of the Empty Quarter it may not rain for years at a time and a single rainfall is considered sufficient to nourish some of the grazing shrubs for four years.

The only wild creatures which can live in the desert are those which can survive with little or no water. A few large animals, notably the gazelle, the oryx, the wolf and the fox, have adapted to drinking rarely and little. Several reptiles live happily in this arid environment. Most common of them are the lizards, which range from tiny, darting creatures to the ungainly *dhub*, some 1m (3ft) from head to tail-tip. Snakes are common in some places and, as several of them are highly poisonous, they are regarded with fear by the bedouin. Another creature to be feared is the scorpion, a small creature with a venomous sting in its curved tail which it flicks up over its back. The sting is painful, though not fatal, to adults, but sometimes causes the death of small bedouin children. Children are particularly vulnerable also to the camel spider, a poisonous insect which finds its way into the tents.

Unlike these wild creatures, men do need water. The bedouin must follow the rain, taking their flocks and herds to areas where rain has fallen and the grazing is good. In autumn, winter and spring, their major preoccupation is to learn, preferably sooner than other bedouin, where the vegetation has grown, since in many areas it is a case of first come first served. They watch for the rain clouds, strange localised clouds in which lightning flashes like the strobe lights in a discothèque, or dark thunderous cloud curtains. Then they send scouts to find whether rain did in fact fall where the lightning flashed. During their winter and spring migrations, some tribes travel 4000km (1,500 miles) or more. The camel herders travel furthest; shepherd tribes move within a smaller area for sheep are dependent on frequent watering and are less mobile.

A winter's drought is the worst disaster which can befall the bedouin. And when the drought is prolonged from one year to the next it can spell ruin and death. Ancient memories of terrible droughts are reflected in the Bible story of the seven lean and seven fat years. In recent times an eight years' drought struck Arabia from the mid-fifties to the mid-

39

sixties. The bedouin herds were decimated and very many bedouin abandoned the nomadic life at that time and settled in the cities. Since then good rains have enabled those who remained to rebuild their animal stocks until, ten years later, they reached or even possibly exceeded the numbers owned before the drought.

When rain does fall it is not always totally benign. Sometimes a year's rainfall or more will pour down in a cloudburst which lasts only a few hours, but which causes highly destructive torrents which can sweep away all in their path. People may drown when too much water falls in the desert, just as they may die when too little causes dehydration. The best known example of such a disaster in recent years happened in the 1950s. A party of tourists was travelling down a narrow gorge in the mountains of Edom in southern Jordan, intending to visit the ancient ruins of Petra, when a sudden storm caused a wall of water, a 'flash flood', to pour down the gorge. All but a couple of the tourists were swept away and drowned. In the same flood waters were found the remains of the last known ostrich in Arabia.

In just a few places in the desert the water from such storms can be used to support vegetation. It seeps undergound and may flow along beneath the beds of *wadis* which can then be cultivated by sinking wells into the water table. These fertile areas, called oases, are to the bedouin as harbours are to mariners. They come here to replenish their supplies, stocking up on dates and grain, tobacco, onions and other vegetables, before setting out for their winter migrations in the high desert. Many bedouin tribes own land in the oases in their home districts; they employ farmers to work it for them and pay these farmers with a share of the produce ($\frac{1}{5} - \frac{1}{3}$ of the dates and most of the vegetables). In late summer, at the time of the date harvest, the bedouin camp in large numbers around the oases, and the date gardens are a hive of activity.

In some oases malaria and other fevers made year-long settlement difficult, but in the more healthy ones permanent human habitation goes back to extremely ancient times, and they are often the site of ruins of antique dams, castles or other fortifications. Protection of their vital supply base has always ranked high in the interests of the tribes, as well as of the sedentary farmers who lived there.

The date palm is the basis of desert agriculture. It is a tree which tolerates both very little and very brackish water in a way which no other can. The fruit is nourishing for both men and animals (dates are fed to horses and dogs in the desert), and the yield can be as high as 90kg (200lb) of fruit per annum per tree in the best oases of the Sahara. In most cases irrigation channels bring water to the base of the trees, but in one oasis in the northern Sahara a different method is used: deep pits are dug and the trees planted in these, at a depth where their roots will reach down to the underground water table. For the desert dweller it is as common to look across the tops of the date trees (growing either in a *wadi* or in such pits) as it is to look up into their branches.

The cultivation of vegetables and grain often depends on the date palms also, for the former are commonly grown in the shade beneath them and would rapidly wither if exposed to the full glare of the sun. Within the confines of the oases, a highly intensive land use has thus been devised and this is now being transferred to other desert areas brought recently under cultivation by means of deep wells worked by motor pumps.

Outside the oases, vegetation is poor and concentrated where the rainfall is highest, or along the courses of *wadis* where there is underground water to which trees and shrubs can drop their roots. Most desert plants have very long roots and very little foliage, to economise on evaporation. Many have thorns or prickles which only the camel will tackle. Most colourful is the oleander, a poisonous bush whose pink flowers brighten the courses of many *wadis* in the Middle East.

While the nomads' herds can eke an existence out of such unappetising vegetation, they must still have water to sustain them particularly in the summer. In winter, when the grazing is good and the camels are giving milk freely, men and camels can live in the high desert with no water at all. But for the rest of the year water is vital. The source of this water lies underground, in reservoirs in the geological strata which are sometimes of very ancient origin. The water now being tapped from deep levels 1,200m (1,400yd) down around the city of Riyadh, for instance, is over 30,000 years old.

Traditionally the bedouin have always owned wells in the desert.

They do not know who made them, but are certain that they are very old. 'From the days of ignorance' they say; that is, from before the time of Islam. Their wells may be as much as 50m (55yd) deep and water either has to be drawn up by hand in buckets, or an animal may haul a rope which runs over a pulley and raises the bucket. Such wells may flow all day, or may run dry after being worked for a couple of hours. In times of drought travellers have died because the wells for which they were heading were dry.

The tribes, or sections of tribes, who own the various wells in their home area retreat to them in summer. Other tribes are allowed to use them only with permission of the owners, and use of wells has led to many disputes in the past. During recent years, therefore, the governments of the regions have taken advantage of the modern drilling technology at their disposal to dig deep wells for the bedouin. These wells are often worked by pumps and as they are controlled by the government they are free for use by all bedouin.

Establishment of these new, deep wells has solved the disputes over water, and in many cases little townships have sprung up around them. There is some hope that many such wells may become centres for small, semi-sedentary communities of nomads, where they can be provided with a school, a clinic, police station and other services. They have how-

14 Trucks are now often used to transport animals to market and new grazing (*author*)

ever, already attracted more nomads than the land around them can often support. Today, the bedouin who rely more and more heavily on pick-up trucks in their herding, tend to establish their flocks of sheep in the neighbourhood of a well and fetch water to them in oil drums carried in the backs of their trucks – it is less tiring to make a trip of up to 70km (40 miles) a day to cart water than to move a whole flock. As a result the ground is often grazed bare for some 70km around the well.

Not only here is the grazing in the desert deteriorating. In the past each tribe laid claim to an area which it regarded as its home, its *dira*, the district to which it retreated in summer or in time of trouble. The tribes managed the grazing in their own *dira* carefully because they might need it in emergency, and other tribes were excluded or paid rent if they were allowed in. In recent years governments have stopped the fighting in the deserts and thrown open the grazing land, protected by a system known as *hema*, to all comers. As a result tribes have taken less interest in managing their grazing. National frontiers have had a similar effect: the tribes cross the frontiers happily to graze their flocks and herds but feel no responsibility for the state of the grazing on the other side. Widespread use of desert shrubs as fuel for fires and cooking also causes a deterioration of the vegetation which could eventually lead to erosion.

As well as the pick-up trucks, the bedouin today often also own (or can hire) heavy trucks into which their flocks and herds can be loaded and moved in a few hours to good grazing elsewhere. In this way the best grazing is eaten off very quickly as it does not have time to become established before the flocks are there, unlike in the old days when it might take days or weeks for the flocks to reach a good grazing area.

It is not only the domestic animals whose lives have been radically altered by the use of motor vehicles in the desert. The wild animals of the region have, in many cases, been virtually wiped out. Until the early days of this century, the deserts were well stocked with herds of gazelle; there were oryx (a larger animal with a black-and-white striped face and long straight horns, believed to be the origin of the unicorn legend), ostrich, panthers, jackals, hyenas, wolves and foxes, as well as smaller animals—hares, rabbits, jerboas, etc.

Desert animals depend for their survival on a camouflage colouring (almost all of them are sandy coloured) and on their ability to outrun pursuit. In the days when the bedouin hunted them from horseback the chances of escape were even. A long patient pursuit might result for the bedouin in game for his pot. The gazelles and oryx, which were hunted for meat, began to decline in number with the widespread use of the rifle. In the past few decades they have been destroyed by hunting parties running them down in cars and indiscriminately eliminating them with sub-machine guns. The bedouin, who relied on gazelle and oryx for an occasional meal of meat, feel that their desert has been depleted by townsmen coming out in hunting parties with their cars and guns. They report seeing dozens of carcases left to rot in the sun after such hunting expeditions, shooting not for food but simply for sport.

Hunting in the deserts of Arabia now is illegal, but the oryx and ostrich are already extinct in the wild (though a herd of oryx is being built up in captivity in Qatar), and the gazelle has become very rare. The other animals have suffered too, and now are rarely seen. The present prohibition on hunting should increase the chances of survival of the remaining larger desert animals and it has at least reduced hunting for sport, although it is extremely difficult to enforce in the empty spaces of the desert. Governments of desert states are beginning to co-operate with naturalists in attempting to study, preserve and re-establish the beautiful wildlife which once roamed freely in the desert habitat.

3

THE DESERT ECONOMY OF BYGONE DAYS

While man can live moderately comfortably along the fringes of the desert by herding sheep and goats, or in oases by cultivating the date palms, he can barely exist in the inner desert without the camel. Desert dwellers must not only be accomplished camel breeders, they also need to be able to exploit the animal's every potential if they aspire to any but the most precarious and poverty-stricken of existences.

The one-humped camel is native to the deserts of the Middle East and there are many shreds of evidence to show that man had domesticated the camel there by the early second millenium BC. A cuneiform list of rations from Alalakh in north Syria in the eighteenth century BC includes 'one measure of fodder for the camel'. Even firmer evidence comes from Mesopotamian cylinder seal, dated between 1800 and 1400 BC, which shows two riders perched on the back of a camel.

Many stories from the Old Testament mention camels in this period, but they have been thought to be anachronisms; perhaps a camel was substituted for some other animal by a scribe writing hundreds of years after the event, at a time when camels certainly were used. Even if camels were not used in the early second millenium in the Holy Land, they were certainly used elsewhere in the Arabian peninsula, and Richard Bulliet concludes that they were probably first domesticated in southern Arabia. This may have been as early as 2500 BC, he says.

It is certainly in southern Arabia that a profitable use for the camel was found by the end of the second millenium. At that time camel caravans began to trek regularly from the lands of frankincense and myrrh in southern Arabia to the wealthy lands near the Mediterranean. The first historical account of these caravans is the story of the Queen of Sheba who journeyed north to visit King Solomon in the tenth century BC: 'And she came to Jerusalem with a very great train, with camels that bare spices, and very much gold and precious stones.'

Meanwhile camels were beginning to be bred in the deserts in large numbers. The records of the great Assyrian empire, centred in northern Mesopotamia, give the clearest accounts of their presence. The Assyrians fought against all their neighbours at one time or another, and it was inevitable that they should fight the desert nomads as soon as these became a noticeable force. The records of Shalmaneser III in the ninth century tell of a battle at Karkar against Gindibu the Arabian, in which the latter fielded a thousand camel riders. A century later, booty which included 30,000 camels was taken from the Arab queen, Samsi.

Such records mark the beginnings of a desert economy which survived intact until the present century. Of earlier life in the deserts there are no written records, but there may be a living one in the Sulubba.

The Sulubba

At the bottom of the bedouin social scale are the Sulubba, or Sulaib as they are also called. They are a tribe of tinkers, hunters and trackers, who live, not together as strong and powerful tribes do, but each family apart, attached to some branch of another tribe, or wandering between tribes. They perform small services for the bedouin, mending pots and pans, making wooden vessels and saddle-trees, acting as guides in hunting parties or raids. They also serve as entertainers: their women will dance before men, and even with men, and the Sulubbi earn a few sous too by playing the *rababah*, singing, and reciting poetry.

No Arab would dream of marrying a Sulubbi girl (even if he did, his family would certainly forbid it), though he might take one as his mistress for they are particularly beautiful, some having blue eyes and red hair. The Sulubbi men talk in a cringing, whining tone in their dealings with the bedouin, while their women and children may beg when in dire need – an indignity to which no bedouin would stoop.

But a bedouin in trouble is glad of Sulubbi skills. He knows that a poor Sulubbi family would always take in a wounded raider and tend him until he was better – more effectively perhaps than his own people might. Doughty told of a Sulubbi whose wife was bitten on the leg by a poisonous snake and who immediately tied a ligature above the knee and sucked out the venom; the woman survived. Such treatment, Doughty wrote, was unknown to the bedouin.

Perhaps such skills led the bedouin to believe that the Sulubba have supernatural powers, can cast the evil eye, work spells, and produce love potions. Many stories were told in the desert of Sulubbi women who made the course of love run true for a young bedouin man or maid with their potions, but they were somewhat feared for all that. One such story is told here.

A young Rwala chief fell in love with a beautiful girl, but his young wife, the mother of his two little sons, was jealous. She went to a Sulubbi woman for help and the latter asked her to bring a piece of wool from the sheep slaughtered on her husband's wedding day, but to dip it first in the blood of the sheep. The Sulubbi woman mumbled spells over the wool and told the young wife to press it well every Friday until her husband should divorce his new wife.

The husband returned to his first wife after midnight on his wedding night, looking angry. The same thing happened each night for two weeks, until he beat his new wife and divorced her. With her he had been impotent, and the bride returned to her parents a virgin. The Sulubbi spell had had its effect.

The Sulubba earn a meagre living by these small services to the bedouin, but much of the time they must support themselves. They travel light, with a tiny skin tent for shelter, keeping only donkeys for their support. They are better hunters than any bedouin, creeping up to their game, covered sometimes in a gazelle skin to prevent their quarry scenting them. They know all the paths of the wild beasts, and can track their prey across the desert with astounding skill.

On the move they carry no supplies other than a very little water and an old rifle. Nor do they count on using the bedouins' great wells. They have a secret knowledge of the desert, of little water holes unknown to the bedouin which enable them to go into the remotest areas. They also have survival techniques superior to those of the bedouin. Doughty noticed that the Sulubba drank their fill two hours before dawn and could then go until noon without further drink. He tried this on a long march and found that he also could wait until noon for water, while his bedouin companions had to drink three times.

Since the Sulubba pay but lip-service to Islam, have a non-Muslim attitude to women (they are monogamous and their women are relatively free), a non-Semitic appearance and traces of foreign roots in their speech, it has long been recognised that they are 'different'. The desert Arabs claim the Sulubba are either of ancient stock or descendants of the Crusaders, an idea supported by their cross-mark *wasm* (brand-mark) and their name, for *Sulaib* means 'little cross'. It has also been suggested that they were a kind of gipsy from India, but their blood groups were found to be very different from those of Indians, rather different from European ones, and most similar to those of Arabs, according to Dr Giraud. It is therefore most likely that they come from ancient desert stock.

The Caravan Trade

When camel caravans first became important, around 1000 BC, the lands of southern Arabia were producing large quantities of frankincense and myrrh. These aromatics were much in demand by the rich civilisations of the Mediterranean littoral for religious ritual. The route between producer and market was long and hard: seafaring was dangerous, and pirates added to the hazards. Overland there were long stretches of desert without water. Only the camel offered the possibility of bringing the goods to their markets.

For hundreds of years the south Arabian states flourished on their control of the caravan trade. They developed a luxurious civilisation which led the Romans to name their lands *Arabia Felix*, 'Happy Arabia'. In time other people along the route wanted a share in the caravan profits. The first to do anything about this were a nomad tribe of the Hejaz called the Nabataeans.

They established themselves in the rocky stronghold of Petra, in the mountains of Edom, at a crossroads on the caravan route. They built up an emporium for trade, policed the routes, and ensured water supplies at Petra. In return they extracted tolls of 25 per cent of the value of the merchandise. By thus establishing themselves profitably as policemen of the caravan routes, they set a precedent which was to be followed by desert nomads for more than 2,000 years. Although the Nabataeans themselves eventually succumbed to the expansion of the Roman empire and changing trade routes, and their present-day descendants are thought to be the ordinary tribe of Huwaytat, their mantle (in the form of control of the incense trade) fell some centuries later on another Arab tribe, the Quraish, who made their headquarters half way along the trade route, at an oasis called Mecca.

Their influence was to be more far reaching than that of the Nabataeans, for among them was born the Prophet Muhammad, founder of the religion of Islam and the man the welded the desert tribes together to produce a force which, radiating from Mecca, was to conquer an empire as widespread as that of the Romans.

In that expansion the Arab tribes crossed the other great Near Eastern desert, the Sahara, peopled already by the nomad Tuareg. In the following centuries the Arabs established themselves there, alongside the Tuareg, as controllers of the rich Saharan caravan routes which brought gold and slaves from the lands south of the Sahara in exchange for salt produced in more northerly areas of the desert. The nomads' role was the same in Arabia: they offered protection in exchange for a fee, provided camels as beasts of burden, sold their services as guides and, when a caravan refused their tolls, made an even greater profit by raiding it.

That breeding camels for these caravans must have provided the nomads with an important income is indicated by the numerous tales of disastrous losses brought back by European travellers in the past century. The earliest of these is an account by an American ship's captain, James Riley, who was shipwrecked off the coast of Morocco and taken as a

slave. In about 1800 he accompanied a caravan across the Sahara to Timbuctoo. A thousand men and 4,000 camels set out from Morocco, but
some way out they were struck by a sandstorm in which 300 men and
200 camels perished. There followed a long waterless stretch of desert
track, on which another 100 men and 300 camels died, before they
reached the only wells available. On arrival they found the wells were
dry. The leaders of the caravan ordered that most of the camels be killed,
since they would not survive the next stretch and could provide nourish-
ment, but no one wanted his own camel killed. In the ensuing fight over
which to kill, between 200 and 300 men and some 500 camels died.

The survivors set off, waterless, to attempt to struggle through to
Timbuctoo. Only twenty-one men and twelve camels eventually
arrived; fortunately for history, one of them was James Riley. That this
was not an exceptional occurrence is borne out by the record of another
caravan, in 1805, going from Timbuctoo to Marrakesh, during which
2,000 men and 1,800 camels perished of thirst in the desert. Indeed, many
of the Saharan caravan routes were said to be marked along much of
their length by the bones of camels and men who had not survived to the
end of the trail.

Camel-breeding

While policing, guiding and raiding desert caravans produced at some
times and in some places a useful (and even luxurious) income for the
bedouin, the main staple of their economy always lay in breeding and
herding. Lesser tribes bred sheep and goats along the fringes of the
desert, but the great bedouin tribes concentrated on camels both as a
source of strength and as a source of income.

Their herding was based on their own tribal lands, known as the *dira*.
These were extensive ranges held by tradition and force, and their size
depended on the strength of the tribe and the richness, or otherwise, of
the grazing available. The ranges could be very vast: that of the Al
Murrah which incorporates the barren sand dunes of the Empty
Quarter, is the size of France. Within its boundaries the tribe and its
various sections owned the wells to which they retreated during the summer.

Tribes were not confined to their own *dira*, however. They moved out into other parts of the desert following the winter rains and the spring grazing, sometimes travelling 1,500 miles or so in a year. When they moved thus, they would ask permission of other tribes to cross their land, or to stay and graze there. Friendly tribes would grant this permission, charging a small fee for the privilege. Fathers Jaussen and Savignac found that the Fuqara tribe and their neighbours charged a rent of 1 megidy (then a little less than $1) per tent in the early part of this century.

However, if a tribe would not grant access to its land to another tribe, conflict and war could ensue. In the early 1920s, the Rwala, driven to despair by severe drought, marched without permission into the *dira* of the Fidan tribe. The Rwala expected war, which in their weakened state would have been very terrible; fortunately for them, a peaceful settlement was negotiated in the nick of time.

The bedouin lived largely off their camels, and the main element of their diet was camel's milk. The camels were also a source of meat, but the bedouin did not often kill an adult one. The adult camel gives as much meat as seven sheep, but it is rather tough; more often the bedouin ate the young male camels, which were usually slaughtered soon after birth.

It it not easy to calculate how many camels were kept in the deserts in the past. Most travellers agree, however, on the numbers of camels per tent, which ranged from an average of about fifty for rich tribes down to about twenty for poor tribes. Less than twenty was distinctly poor. In the late-nineteenth century, for example, Doughty wrote that the Fuqara (whose name means 'the poor ones') had 200 households and barely 1,500 camels between them. The average for the same period for the great tribes of the Anazah confederation was fifty per household, and for the Huwaytat and Shararat it was twenty.

However, to deduce from this the total number of camels in Arabia, one would need to know the total number of households per tribe, and here figures vary widely. Carl Raswan reckoned the Rwala tribe alone to have 300,000 camels in the 1920s, and his estimate of 50,000 tents for the tribes of northern Arabia and Syria would give a figure of around

15 The camel is still an important means of travel in the desert, although the use of trucks is increasing (*Barnaby's*)

one and a quarter million camels.

Marketing the camels was a highly organised affair. The markets for the camels bred in the deserts of Arabia were the towns of Egypt, Syria and Iraq, but the bedouin themselves had nothing to do with that aspect of camel rearing. They were visited in the deserts by professional merchants known as the *Uqail,* whose headquarters were in Baghdad and who had handled the camel trade since time immemorial. The *Uqail* were aware of the fluctuations in camel prices (which depended on such alien factors as the fluctuation in the value of the cotton crop in Egypt, for example), and set their price each season accordingly. In the last century this price would be paid part in cash, part in calico for the bedouin's long gowns.

The bedouin's main income, then, was from the sale of the camels. It was, however, an income which was very much a hostage to fortune. Not only could their own herds be drastically reduced by drought, leaving them with only poor, thin animals for sale, or even no surplus at all; but the price which they fetched was also subject to fluctuations in the world economy, over which the unfortunate bedouin had no control. In good times things went well, however: in the 1870s, for instance, Doughty mentioned that the price of camels had doubled within the past few years. During World War I the price again went up, doubling or trebling from pre-war days.

That was the last of the good times, however, so far as the sale of camels was concerned. After the war prices fell to rock bottom and, in the 1920s, a camel which had fetched £50–100 during the war, could bring in only £3–6. The bedouin lost their income from camels and, by the 1930s, they were reduced to extreme poverty. Their main market for sale, Egypt, had virtually ceased to buy from Arabia and was importing from the Sudan instead. At that time poor bedouin families were said to be living on an annual income of £10, and some had no income at all.

Fortunately for the bedouin, most tribes owned one other source of food supply apart from their camels, and that was land in the oases. The bedouin did not themselves work on this land, but employed slaves or peasants to cultivate it for them, and at harvest time they moved down to the oases to claim their share of the crop. A date palm produces between 18 and 90kg (40–200lb) of dates per year; of this the cultivator would keep one-third, and the bedouin took two-thirds to provide their main source of solid food for the year. Beneath the date palms the cultivators managed vegetable gardens in which they grew cereals, vegetables and tobacco. Most of this crop they kept for themselves, since it was highly seasonal, but the bedouin landowners received supplies of grain and a little of the other crops too. The dates are still important to the bedouin today, and at harvest time their tents are pitched around the oases, or they move into recently built shacks on the outskirts of the cultivation. After the harvest the bedouin return to the desert, often taking with them the cultivators' flocks which they will care for during the good grazing season in winter and spring.

Finally, strong (or well placed) tribes could count on a certain income from *khuwa*. *Khuwa*, the tax of 'brotherhood', was in fact a kind of protection money which strong bedouin extorted from weak tribes, villagers and travellers and caravans, for protection from themselves and other strong bedouin. Doughty tells of three Billi tribesmen who arrived 'driving a few sheep in discharge of a *khuwa*, or debt for "brotherhood", to the Fukara, for safe conduct of late, which was but to come in to traffic at the hajj market'. The Fuqara were not a strong tribe, but the Billi were even weaker.

Villagers and settled folk were harassed for *khuwa* especially when the central government was weak, in which case the tribes' demands became at times so excessive that the villagers were forced to abandon their fields to the nomads. When the central government was strong, fewer villagers and weak tribes were ready to pay.

Merchant caravans generally found it worthwhile to pay the tolls demanded by the bedouin. A small well armed guard could, in practice, often beat off a much larger force of bedouin intent on pillage, but, by and large, caravans found it preferable to pay the tolls for a peaceful journey. The same was true of the great annual pilgrimage, the *hajj*, to Medina and Mecca. In the last century and the early years of this one, the Turkish government paid a generous subsidy to the tribes along the pilgrim route, for safe conduct for the pilgrims. When, for some reason, the subsidy was not paid in a given year, the bedouin attacked and looted several of the forts which safeguarded the pilgrims' night halts.

In the present century, however, strong central governments were established in all the Arab states. Even the small states began to resist the demands for *khuwa*. Dickson tells how the Ajman and Bani Hajir tribes once blockaded Kuwait because merchants there refused to pay them *khuwa*. The ruler of Kuwait retaliated by preventing the Ajman tribesmen from coming into his market, and arranging with two other towns to do the same thing.

Tougher measures by far were taken by Abd al Aziz Ibn Saud, the determined desert leader who conquered and united the present kingdom of Saudi Arabia. One of his early measures was to prohibit the demanding of *khuwa* altogether. How he enforced his commands we shall see in Chapter 8.

4

BEDOUIN ECONOMY TODAY

Oh the full bucket,
May Allah save it from the sides of the well.
He shall not water his camel
Who does not pull up the bucket well. . . .
The need of the camels
On the day at the well
Is for two slaves and a master.
If one slave tires
Not so the Master.

A camel-watering song from Musil

The Camel

The camel has always been the mainstay of the bedouin economy. Indeed, the name 'bedouin', strictly speaking, applies only to tribes who keep camels and are of noble descent. Nowadays we tend to use the term 'bedouin' rather loosely, to describe all the Arab nomads of the desert; but the bedouin themselves are more precise. For them settled tribesmen are *hadari*, nomadic sheep herders and lesser tribes are *arab*, and noble camel herding tribes are *badawyin* (bedouin).

The camel of the Arabian deserts is the single-humped dromedary, as distinct from the two-humped Bactrian camel of Asia. The Arabian camel has shorter hair and longer legs than the Asian variety; it can tolerate extreme heat but would not thrive in the cold, as the Bactrian camel does in the mountains of central Asia.

The number of camels in the Middle East has diminished rapidly in recent years, as the car and truck have taken over its role in transport. There can be only estimates of the numbers surviving today but these at least provide some indication. The Food and Agriculture Organisation (FAO) estimated in 1973 that there were nearly 600,000 camels in Saudi Arabia, 8,000 in Syria, 18,000 in Jordan and 38,000 in Iraq. Very large herds of camels are still bred in the Sudan and Somalia and these countries now export camels to the Arab lands to their north.

In the inner desert the bedouin depend for their lives on their camels, and the animal is equally dependent on his master. A close relationship exists between man and beast; although, to the outsider, the camel is far from elegant and has a very strong and disagreeable smell, to the bedouin he is beautiful. His name, camel (*jamal* in Arabic), comes from the same root as 'beautiful' (*jamil*). He has very many other names as well; there is a different word for a camel in virtually every year and state of his life. It is often claimed, in fact, that every Arabic word has one basic meaning, an opposite meaning, and a meaning which has something to do with a camel.

Camels vary in quality and beauty just as horses do. The best are those from the south, known as Omanis. Like horses, they are judged by their good points: a fine she-camel has small pointed ears, shining eyes, small feet and long slim legs, an arched neck, broad ribs and chest, and her hump immediately above her abdomen. If the camel is in good condition the hump is firm – the animal stores its fat in its hump and when it is in poor condition, or has gone hungry for some time, the hump shrinks.

The bedouin are very interested in the colour of their camels and breed herds especially to retain a favourite colour. In the north of Arabia, Syria and Jordan, the favourite colour is white and great prestige is attached to white herds. In the past these were the prime target of camel raiders and their recovery was the first concern of those who had been raided. White camels were in fact less useful than coloured ones

16 Bedouin from Morocco loading their camels on an Atlantic trade route to the desert

since they could not be used in raids because they were so visible in the desert; nevertheless those that were pure white, without a single black hair, were the pride of their owners and their hair the source of the finest woven goods. In the south of Arabia, however, black or very dark brown are the prestigious colours for camels, and black herds are the treasured ones. The Al Murrah of the Empty Quarter, who own a fine black herd, claim that it descends from black camels taken in raids in the last century from the Mutayr tribe. As the Al Murrah were able to retreat into the sands of their desolate home territory they were able to avoid pursuit and keep the black camels.

Camels can survive for long periods without water, and it is this ability which makes them the main support of bedouin life in the inner desert. In winter, when the grazing is fresh and the temperature moderate, a camel may go a month or six weeks with no water. In spring they can survive for a week or ten days, but in summer they must be watered every two or three days and can drink 25 gallons of water at a time when they have gone thirsty for a while. Their body is particularly adapted to the desert: their rate of water loss is less than a third that of the average mammal and their body heat can vary by $12F°$ ($6C°$) without causing them trouble; they do not sweat at temperatures below $105°F$ ($40°C$). Their endurance is increased by their ability to store liquid in their stomachs. The bedouin know of this and, in the last extremities of thirst, will kill a camel and drink the liquid from its belly.

Females have greater endurance than males and are therefore used exclusively as riding camels, while the males if kept at all are kept as beasts of burden. A female camel has great courage and will keep going until she drops dead of exhaustion or thirst; when very thirsty, however, she moans pitiably and tears roll down her cheeks.

For the bedouin, the camel's most important product is her milk. A camel on good grazing will suckle her own young and give 4 or 5 litres (1 gal) a day for her owner's use. Camel milk is the staple fare of the bedouin diet; many of their meals consist solely of milk and they live for days on end on little else. It is often made into a rather liquid yogurt of which the bedouin are particularly fond.

Camel meat is a great treat for a bedouin family. They usually enjoy it only on special occasions, at times of festivals, rejoicing, or the visit of a guest. It is generally a young male camel which is slaughtered as females are rarely killed. Adult animals are sold to the town markets for meat, but the bedouin themselves do not often eat adult camels which are tougher than young ones. From the fat of a slaughtered camel suet is made which can be kept for many months. It enriches a meal of bread or rice, and as it is cooling, is especially favoured in summer.

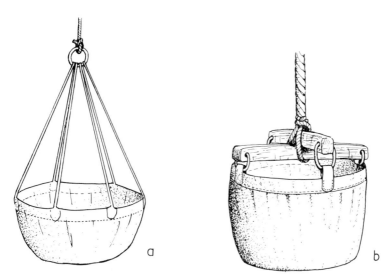

17 a) leather bucket used for raising water; b) bucket made from car tyre inner tube and held rigid with cross pieces of wood, also used for raising water

The camel's hair is used for weaving bags and plaiting ropes, and its hide is made into leather pouches, especially water bags. Its dung provides a staple fuel for the camp fire, or may be ground up and used as a paste for medicinal purposes. A baby's hips may be plastered with dry dung to act as a nappy. Even the urine is used by the bedouin who collect it and wash their hair in it – this is an effective way of killing head lice and leaves the hair black and shiny.

A female camel may begin to breed from the age of six years. She carries her calf for twelve months and suckles it for a further twelve. The baby camel is born with a woolly coat, but by the end of the first year it has lost most of this, retaining only a woolly tuft, soon to disappear, at the top of its hump. A camel's life span is not very different from that of a horse and it may live to be over twenty years old.

Camels are carefully bred to ensure that the young will be born at a suitable time of the year, usually in the winter. Each herd has a few male animals kept as beasts of burden and for breeding. During the rutting season the males are kept tied up until a female is brought to them. Some bedouin are superstitious about the days on which their camels are mated, preferring a Friday or Sunday to other days.

The herds are owned by the family group. The senior man, father, or grandfather is, strictly speaking, the owner of the family's assets which he holds in trust for the others. Young men who have earned money working in the town, or elsewhere, spend it to supplement the family's herds rather than breaking out on their own. Average herds consist of around forty or fifty camels, but poorer nomads with small families may manage with less, and rich shaikhs own many more.

Mark	Name	Mark	Name
+	Awazim	⅂.	Ajman (known as Al Zézé)
⟑	Subah (Kuwait)	·Π	Sa'aran (Mutair)
⚲	Sufran (Ajman)	⚲	Al Saleh (Ajman)
ıU	Al Huwaila (Ajman)	ϙ	Al Dha'in (Ajman)
·ǀ·	Hithlain	·ǁ	Ibn Aisdan (Sulaiman - Ajman)
U	Salim al Hamud (one of Al Subah Shaikhs)	ǁ	Ibn Rashidan (Mutair)
∓	Qahtan (also Utaybah)	ǀ.	As Sur (Mutair)
++	Utaybah	T	Ibn Shuwairibat - Braih (Mutair)
ǀoǀ	Ajman	Π	Ibn Jáma (Awazim)
		⌒	Ibn Drai (Awazim)

18 *Wasm* marks

60

Camels are branded with the owner's mark, called the *wasm*, just as, for instance, New Forest ponies are branded in England. The *wasm* is a geometric sign — circle, arrow, cross, dot, etc. — and the position in which it is branded on the animal's hide also helps indicate ownership. There are literally thousands of different *wasms* in the desert. A very few tribes have one brand mark for the whole tribe; most tribes have a large number and the marks indicate related families, close relatives having similar though slightly different marks. The *wasm* is sometimes chipped into the rocks in tribal territory, or marked on goods temporarily abandoned in the desert, to indicate ownership.

The camels spend the night hobbled near their owner's tent, but in the daytime they are taken out to grass. Early in the morning the camel-herder releases the rope on each camel's legs (hobbling is done by tying the forelegs together just above the foot, or by tying one foreleg up to the knee) and leads the camels out in a long line to find fresh grazing. In the evening he brings them back to the tent just before nightfall, singing to them to encourage them to keep moving.

When the camels come back to the tents at night they are milked by the men. During the daytime a bag is placed over the female camel's udders and tied above the hump with cords; this prevents the young from suckling. When the bag is slid up to one side the young camels can suckle and the mother is milked while the young one is still near, for she will not give milk unless her baby is close to her. In the past the milk was collected in wooden milking bowls. Today it is more often taken in a plastic jerry-can.

Camel herding involves continual movement for the bedouin who cannot stay in one place for any length of time if their herds are to find sufficient food. For most of the year the nomads must move their tents every week or ten days, in a permanent quest for grazing. Only in summer, when they camp by their tribal wells in order to have the water they need for survival, do the bedouin stay for any length of time in one place. Then they may camp for three or four months in close company with scores, perhaps hundreds, of other tents. The start of the summer camp is a period of great excitement, visits to relatives and friends, and feasting. But as the long hot months drag on, the nomads, who are used to a relatively quiet and solitary life in small groups in the desert, begin to find that so many relatives get on their nerves. Tempers fray and they are glad when the autumn rains come and they can move off again, back to a genuinely nomadic life.

During autumn, winter and spring the bedouin may travel hundreds of kilometres by easy stages, following the rainclouds. The decision is taken early in the morning for the camping group to move; tents are then lowered, belongings packed onto the baggage camels, and the women and small children climb up into their basket-work litters. These litters are made of local wood, usually tamarisk or pomegranate, and are draped with brightly coloured cloths to shelter the women riding in them. They are made in different styles by the different tribes, the most spectacular being the great winged litters of the Anazah. These litters, when swaying high above a camel and draped in bright materials, have the appearance of huge fluttering butterflies moving slowly across the desert. Today, however, this picturesque sight is becoming rarer for, in practice, it is much more comfortable to bump across the desert in a truck than to sway for hours in a litter. Families are making increasing use of small pick-up trucks which they load up in incredible fashion with tent and belongings, brushwood, animals, barrels of water, pots and pans and – on top of it all – the children. Or, for their major migrations, they may use large lorries which they can rent if they do not own one.

The camel was undisputedly the best means of travelling in the desert before the days of cars and trucks. It is capable of amazing endurance and a useful turn of speed, although in this it cannot rival the horse. A camel galloping flat out, with her neck stretched out before her rather like a swan in flight, will travel at over 20km (12 miles) an hour. If pushed she can keep up a high speed for many hours; there are stories of camels travelling 150–200km (90–125 miles) a day for several days on end and, alas, often dropping dead on arrival at their destination.

A female riding camel, called *dhalul* by the bedouin, is carefully trained by her owner. She must be taught to kneel for him to mount and to rise only when he is firmly in his seat; she rises first on her forelegs then on her hind ones, like an abrupt rocking horse. Unless she is well

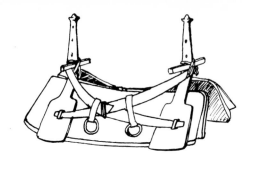

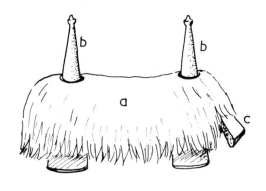

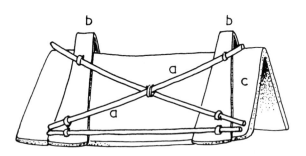

19 Camel saddles: (top) riding saddle (uncovered); (centre) riding saddle (a) sheepskin covering (b) pommels (c) leather cushion for resting leg on when crossed in front of the saddle; (above) common pack saddle (a) cross-pieces attached to saddle arches (b) and (c) weight-carrying pads (*after Dickson*)

trained she begins to move as soon as she feels the rider's weight, and this can give him an awkward moment. She must also be taught to move at a comfortable pace, to turn at the tap of a stick on her neck, and to stop at the click of a tongue. Camels are not bridled like horses; the rider's only physical control is a cord around her muzzle, or fixed to a ring in her nose. In effect she is controlled by her rider's voice.

The camel is not an easy animal to saddle: where the horse has a good straight back on which a saddle can conveniently be placed, the camel has a hump. The hump has no bone structure; it consists of fat and cannot alone support the weight of a saddle. On the other hand there is rather little space, either before or behind the hump, on which to place a saddle. Over the years, and in the various deserts of the Middle East, various methods of riding the camel have been tried. In southern Arabia bareback riders kneel behind the hump; in the Sahara the Tuareg sit on a small saddle perched before the hump.

The most widespread and successful system of saddling came from northern Arabia. This saddle is called the *shadād* (which means 'strong one'). It consists of a rigid, wooden saddle-tree which is supported on the camel's ribcage. A cushion stuffed with camel hair is placed under the saddle tree on either side of the hump, and further small cushions, sheep skins, and woven cloths are placed over the wooden frame for comfort and decoration. Sometimes the pommel of the frame is decorated with silver to make it yet more attractive. This saddle serves a second purpose as an armrest on which the men lean while sitting round the coffee fire in their tents.

The bedouin are expected to pay an alms tax, called *zakat*, on the camels and other livestock which they own. This tax is collected during the summer camp at their wells, and is paid in livestock: in Saudi Arabia it is one ewe for each five camels owned, excluding the first five on which nothing is paid. On the other hand they may receive a govern-

20 A market town in the Algerian Sahara. Nomads have brought their flocks into the oasis market to sell (*author*)

ment subsidy in cash for the animals they keep. Again in Saudi Arabia this amounts to about 20 riyals (£3.40) per sheep, and 50 riyals (£8.50) per camel per year.

Sheep-breeding

Very many desert nomads breed sheep instead of, or as well as, camels. The type of sheep found in Arabia is the fat-tailed breed which has been living there for many thousands of years, to judge from ancient rock carvings of the animal. It is usually white or black-and-white in colour; the commonest colour in central Arabia is pure black with a white head and the eyes outlined in black, giving an odd, bespectacled look.

Far more sheep are reared in the deserts than camels. FAO estimates of the numbers in the early 1970s give 3 million sheep in Saudi Arabia, 5.25 million in Syria, 1.2 million in Jordan, and 4.75 million in Iraq. In the past, lesser tribes living on the fringes of the desert were the ones who reared sheep. They were somewhat despised by the noble camel-herding bedouin since they had less power and less wealth. Today, sheep raising is more profitable than camel-herding, and most of the noble tribes are beginning to keep sheep as well as camels. The wealthiest tribes are now those with large flocks of sheep.

The truck has made a great difference to sheep-breeding. Sheep need water daily and could once only be raised on the edges of the desert where there was ready access to water. Today's shepherds can bring water to their flocks and can take their flocks by truck across barren regions which they could not traverse on foot, to find good grazing the other side. New areas of grazing have been opened to them by this increased mobility, and marketing has become much easier also.

The sheep find a ready market in the towns where mutton is more popular than camel meat. A full-grown sheep fetches between £50 and £100, and the income from a flock of sheep can more or less cover the purchase price in one year. Sheep have a shorter gestation period than camels and reach maturity quicker, and many ewes produce twin lambs. A bedouin family can survive with a flock of, say, 50–60 sheep plus a few goats, but it is becoming increasingly difficult for them to do so, since owning a truck can be expensive and they easily fall into debt. In these circumstances they are tending more and more to work for large-scale owners with flocks of hundreds, or even thousands, of sheep.

Unlike camels, which are always cared for and milked by men, sheep are frequently in the charge of the women of the family. The women and children may look after them as they graze, and it may be the women who milk them when they come back to the tents at night. During the daytime the lambs remain by the tents and wander in and out. The little children of the family play with them and the animals become very tame from birth. At night, when the mothers are brought back to the tents, the lambs are already tied up for the night. As each mother is called in turn by her name, her own lamb is brought to her to suckle. Out in the desert sheep and lambs must be tied very close to the tent at night for fear of wolves which will carry off adults and young alike if a close watch is not kept. Bedouin believe that the wolf can understand human speech because he was once human himself and owned all the sheep and goats, but was turned into a wolf for some great sin. A shepherd will sometimes draw a circle around the young animals in his care, to protect them from wolves to whom he addresses the following words: 'The circle of Solomon, son of David, is between thee and me. It thou breakest it, Allah will break thee.'

Sheep-rearing families move far less frequently than camel herders and many of them are really only semi-nomadic. In winter they may take their flocks out to graze in the desert, staying far longer in one place than camel herders. They move perhaps only five or six times throughout the whole cool season. They travel less far also, generally not more than about 200–300km (125–185 miles). For the rest of the year they may live in village houses, their tent folded up in the corner, or they may simply set up their tent in one place and keep it there. Sometimes they use both tent and village house, or tent and shanty, and the two stand side by side.

Such families begin to keep other creatures around their tents. They often have a flock of chickens, small birds almost like bantams who wander into the tents and perch on the piles of belongings. And they may keep a cat which is said to scare away scorpions and snakes. Cats are adaptable, and bedouin cats will happily make a meal of desert lizards, eating up the body and leaving the severed tail to thrash in the sand.

Shepherd families who spend several months in one place often find that they have the time and opportunity to cultivate the land, and they may grow alfalfa for their flocks and some grain for their own travels. They also have time to develop the products of their flocks. The women weave far more than camel-herding women do; they make leather bags, rugs and woven cloth for sale in the town which may not be so far away. And they also make *ghee* (clarified butter), yogurt and a kind of hard, white cheese. Those who live near the towns are beginning to make urban articles such as embroidered cushion covers and cloths; some have hand-operated sewing machines in their tents and make their own clothes.

The Arab Horse

When a recent traveller in the desert asked a bedouin shaikh why he kept a bicycle leaning against his tent-pole rather than an Arab mare, the old man replied sadly: 'Bicycles don't eat.' It is a scene which might have occurred in many bedouin tents throughout the desert, for bikes, motorbikes and pick-up trucks have replaced the horse as rapid means of transport.

Horses were never very common in the desert, and today they are very rare. The amazing thing is that they were bred in the desert at all; it is even more amazing that the purest and best horses in the world were produced there. Horses cannot survive on salty, prickly, tough desert plants, as camels can. They need proper feeding and in the past many bedouin families went hungry to ensure that their mare had enough to eat.

The bedouin kept horses for raiding, warfare and prestige. A fine well bred mare was a source of immense pride and pleasure to her bedouin owner; stallions were rarely kept, colts usually being killed at birth, and the bedouin did not geld. Great care was taken to ensure a good stock: only the best stallions were retained for breeding, and breeding lines of desert horses were remembered for generations back. Mares were mated in front of witnesses, and haphazard breeding was not allowed.

The result of this care was a fine, pure-bred race of horses of great beauty and stamina. When the British aristocracy wanted to improve their own native breeds for racing purposes, there was only one place to look and that was to the deserts of the Middle East and the Arab horses there. Towards the end of the seventeenth century and the beginning of the eighteenth, many fine Arab horses were imported into Britain. The stallions were mated with native mares. Three of them, the Byerley Turk, the Darley Arabian and the Godolphin Barb, are the ancestors of all thoroughbred horses in the world today.

In the desert, mares were fed on camel's milk and dates. Grass is rarely available, and grain is always in short supply, but the Arabs had been encouraged by the Prophet Muhammad to feed their horses well: 'As many grains of barley as thou givest thy horse, so many sins shall be forgiven thee,' he said. Although camels have always been much more useful to the bedouin than horses, a good mare was prized far above a camel. In the past, between fifteen and thirty racing camels might be paid for a fine mare. The Emir Fuaz of the Rwala once offered forty camels for the return of a bloodmare which had been taken in a raid.

While the bedouin will cut the throat of a sheep, goat or camel for meat, without the slightest worry, and will hunt animals and game birds for the pleasure of the sport as well as the meat, they cannot bring themselves to kill an adult horse.

Doughty tells a pathetic story of Shaikh Mahanna's mare which bore a foal in old age but had not the strength to suckle it. The shaikh turned his mare out into the desert, without food or water, and took the foal into his tent to rear it on camel's milk.

The mare roamed sadly around the tents for three days, and the bedouin looked out unhappily every hour to see when she would die. Doughty was shocked at their cruelty and urged them to put her out of her misery with a gunshot, but they were equally appalled by his suggestion. On the third noon the mare fell down from weakness; at dawn the next day they knew her to be dead as the vultures had gathered over her. Only then did the shaikh order the camp to be moved: he would not leave as long as his mare lived.

21 Engraving of the Darley Arabian after a painting by John Wooton (*Fores Ltd*)

This tradition has carried over into the towns of Arabia today. Many large white donkeys are still used to pull carts and, especially, small water tankers. When they are too old or ill to work, their owners can no longer afford to keep them; there is no grazing and everything a donkey eats must be purchased. But the owner will not kill his donkey, nor will a local vet agree to put an animal down. So, old donkeys are simply turned loose into the swirling traffic of the city's streets. Like Mahanna's mare they wander miserably, waterless and foodless, on the burning pavements and busy roads, until they drop with exhaustion or are knocked down by the traffic.

In the past, when Middle Eastern governments were trying to suppress raiding in the deserts, they sought to persuade the bedouin to give up their horses which were kept mainly for that purpose. Such measures as liability to military service for those who owned a mare soon had their effect. Today pure-bred Arab horses live only in the stables of the ruling families; few are to be found around the bedouin tents.

Cash Income

Although the bedouin are virtually self-supporting, they have never been entirely so. Most of their food needs are provided by their animals, or by gardens which they own in oases in their tribal lands, but some things they must buy from the people of the towns. Sale of their own produce does not provide them with a sufficient income to cover all their needs. In the past they needed to buy clothing, weapons including guns and ammunition, coffee, tea, sugar, rice, and some household goods which they bought in the desert from travelling tinkers.

Today their cash needs have risen sharply with the introduction of the widespread use of pick-up trucks and lorries as an integral part of their herding and shepherding practices. Money must be raised for the purchase of the vehicle, for petrol and also for repairs and spare parts. These are a constant problem for desert dwellers, although they themselves are very handy at running repairs to their vehicles. The bedouin standard of living has risen in many other ways as well: they enjoy tinned foods, especially tomato paste and tinned fish, they buy radios, cold boxes, sewing machines, camp cooking-stoves and lamps. They send their children to school and buy medicine for them when they are ill.

The bedouin can raise money for these purchases from a variety of sources. The most important are the governments of the lands in which they live, and paid work in the towns. The various governments pay the bedouin directly for service in the national armies, the National Guard in Saudi Arabia, and the police forces. They also subsidise the tribes with hand-outs on an irregular basis.

Paid employment has attracted a large number of the younger men to work for the oil companies, as seasonal labour, and as truck and taxi drivers. Such young men send remittances to their families living with the tribes, and may return to their tribes themselves when they have raised enough money for a herd of camels or a flock of sheep and a pick-up.

Tribes living along the frontiers have also found that smuggling can provide a useful supplement to their income. The hundreds of miles of desert frontiers are impossible to patrol effectively, and the tribes cross them as of right in the pursuit of grazing. In the 1960s it was estimated that over half the livestock marketed in Libya had been smuggled in by the bedouin. It is a somewhat hazardous occupation, but to the bedouin appears just as legitimate as raiding did in the past.

5
TRIBAL AND SOCIAL STRUCTURE

Bedouin tribes are really rather similar to Scottish clans. Just as members of a Scottish clan have one family name (Campbell, MacDonald, MacIntosh, etc), so the members of a bedouin tribe are, in theory, all related and all descended from some distant ancestor who may well be lost in the mists of time, more imaginary than real. Jaussen and Savignac found that the Fuqara counted their ancestry back eighteen generations to Adam; Cole says the Al Murrah tell of their eponymous ancestor Murrah, who lived before the time of Islam and whose wife was a jinn. Other tribes regard them as noble but slightly tainted by this fairy blood.

In practice, tribes have often absorbed individuals or whole sections of other tribes, but inbreeding produces a close physical relationship within the members of a tribe. Men marry within their own tribe, or, if occasionally they marry outside it, they must choose a bride from a tribe on an equal social footing.

There are around 100 large tribes, of 1,000 members or more in Arabia and neighbouring deserts, and many other tribes in Egypt and the Sahara. Sometimes a tribe will have been divided by the fortunes of grazing or war; one section may be in Iraq or Egypt and another in Arabia. It is difficult to say how large any given tribe is today, since figures are based on estimates and vary widely. There are probably very few really large tribes of 60–70,000 members, far more medium-sized

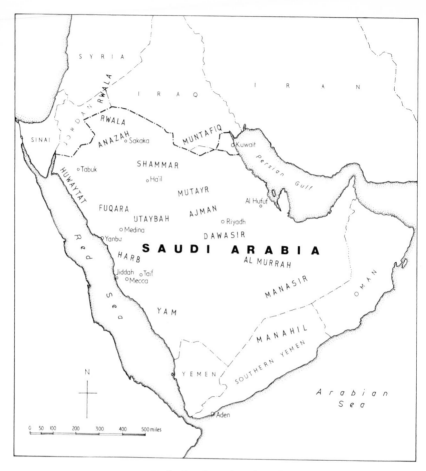

22 Bedouin tribes of Saudi Arabia

tribes of 20–50,000 members, and large numbers of small tribes.

The only tribes which count in the desert as 'bedouin' are camel-herding tribes descended from an ancestor who is generally accepted as noble. Other lesser tribes are known as 'arab' but not bedouin. In practice they may now be richer than the bedouin tribes, but in the past they lacked the power to raid or fight, having no camels, and it was not considered fair play to raid them. Political power rests with the noble tribes, and used to be quite disproportionate to their numbers.

The most powerful tribe in Arabia today is the Anazah. The Anazah is actually more of a federation of tribes for it comprises many distinct tribal units, all of which claim relationship with each other. The largest and most important individual tribe within the Anazah federation, and indeed in the whole of Arabia, is the Rwala with some 75,000 members. The Rwala migrate between the deserts of Syria, Jordan and northern Saudi Arabia, and their paramount shaikh of the Ibn Shaalan family, lives in Damascus.

Two ruling families in the peninsula descend from Anazah tribes. They are the Sabah of Kuwait and the Ibn Saud who have given their name to Saudi Arabia, the kingdom created by Abd al Aziz Ibn Saud after a power struggle with other tribes and settled states in the peninsula.

Ibn Saud's major rival for power in central Arabia in the early part of this century was the great tribe of Shammar with the headquarters of its paramount shaikhs, the Ibn Rashid, at Hail. The Shammar are a very large tribe, comparable to the Rwala, but their leading family wasted its strength around the turn of the century in family assassinations. When the English traveller Gertrude Bell visited Hail before World War I, she found the palace inhabited by young boys and eunuch slaves; all the men of the family had died at the hands of relatives.

The rivalry between the Shammar and the Anazah seems to be inherited from a long-standing split between the tribes of northern Arabia and those of the south, the Yemen. This hostility goes back thousands of years, to before the time of Islam. The Shammar are from the noble Yemeni race, called Qahtan, while the Anazah are from the noble northern race which claims descent from Ishmael.

Beneath the warrings of these noble bedouin tribes the lesser shepherd tribes were left to rear their flocks around the edges of the desert in peace, providing they paid the bedouin for the privilege. Below the shepherd tribes in the social hierarchy of the desert were the Sana, a blacksmith tribe, and Sulubba, a tribe of tinkers and trackers. And beneath them were the negro slaves who were to be found in every bedouin camp. These slaves could rise to positions of considerable power and influence as their masters' confidants, especially when attached to the family of a paramount shaikh. They were treated as the bedouins' own families and held in only nominal captivity since it was very easy for anyone who was not happy to escape to the tents of a rival tribe where he would be freed. Today there are still negroes in the great camps, and they are still called *'abid* (slaves), although they are freemen and simply choose to stay.

The powerful tribes of today are not great tribes of the past. The debris of the great tribes of former times now live a semi-sedentary life around the fringes of the desert, in Iraq and northern Syria. Just as there has been a rise and fall of nation states and political power in Europe over the centuries, so there has been a rise and fall of tribes in Arabia. The desert has limited resources to support its population; when new, large and strong tribes gained power in the central desert, the former masters of the land were pushed out and their tribes broke up.

This movement of tribes, from the south to the north of the peninsula, has been happening since very ancient times. The empires of Assyria and Babylon were established in Mesopotamia by Semitic tribes coming from the deserts to the south. It has led to a continual ebb and flow of populations along the desert borders: tribesmen who had lost their ranges settled; settled folk whose irrigation failed, or who were subject to heavy taxation by the government, moved back to the desert.

The Arab Conquests

The traditional pattern of minor tribal movements was shattered in the seventh century AD. The Prophet Muhammad preached the religion of Islam in Mecca and Medina (in western Arabia) in the early years of that century. His authority was such that he brought the unruly tribes of the desert under his sway during his lifetime. When he died in 632, however, the unity of the tribes began to fragment, and his successor, the Caliph Abu Bakr, had first to subject the tribes and then to find an outlet for their warlike spirit.

His generals led the bedouin out of the peninsula to attack the two great empires to the north of them, Byzantium and Persia. In an amazingly short time the neighbouring countries fell to the dynamic nomad tribes who attacked with zeal in the name of their new religion. By 650 they had conquered the lands which are now Jordan, Israel, Syria, Iraq, Iran and Egypt. The great wave of expansion did not stop there, however. The tribes swept on to take north Africa and Spain, and just one century after the death of their prophet, they were approaching Paris. In a battle which was decisive for the future of Europe, they were at last turned back near Tours by the Frankish leader Charles Martel (Charles the Hammer).

These Islamic conquests carried the name, language and religion of the Arab tribes across a huge empire, a large part of which has remained Arab until the present day. They also gave the bedouin tribes an alternative outlet to their traditional deserts in the Arabian peninsula: the Sahara desert, inhabited already by the Berber Tuareg, was now available to them.

The strangest story in connection with their trek to the west is that of the Beni Hilal. Impoverished remnants of the tribe still live in the mountains of south-western Arabia, in the Asir. Until recently they enjoyed a dubious reputation as robbers and brigands. Today they live in peace but the name of the Beni Hilal still echoes in the Hejaz (western Arabia), their former home; if one asks today who built some great ruined dam or castle, the answer, as likely as not, will be 'the Beni Hilal'. They were thought to have been giants of men: only they could have piled those massive rocks. In fact, like any other nomads, they certainly never built anything of the kind.

To those who read the history of the Maghreb, the name of Beni Hilal rings even more loudly, but with a sinister peal. They descended on the prosperous, cultivated lands of north-west Africa at the turn of the tenth and eleventh centuries like a swarm of locusts. They destroyed all in their path, and civilisation collapsed.

The truth is, perhaps somewhere between. The Beni Hilal took a small part in the Islamic expansions and gained a reputation as the boldest warriors with the longest lances. A few settled in Egypt, and when the rest of the tribe suffered a terrible drought in the Hejaz and their animals and children were dying, others moved in greater numbers to Egypt. They dabbled in troublesome political adventures until the Fatimid Caliph of Egypt was heartily tired of them and banished them to Upper Egypt; but that was still too near to hand.

At this time there was political and religious ferment in the Maghreb, and the Fatimid representatives in Tunisia were murdered. The Caliph's vizier suggested killing two birds with one stone by sending the Beni Hilal to the west. They were headed westwards by the authorities and set off, first in raiding parties and then in tribal groups; within five years the Beni Hilal were masters of the plains of the Maghreb, and were joined by other Arab bedouin, making in all perhaps 200,000 tribesmen. Recent reassessments of the collapse of agriculture in the region following the bedouin invasions suggest that the process may have started before their arrival, and that their victory was facilitated by the decline of the area.

Tribal Structure

The tribe is divided into a number of clans consisting of about 2,000 members each. The chief of one of the more powerful clans will be chosen as the paramount shaikh of the whole tribe and this position may be held by one family for many generations. The clan is an effective political unit; it owns wells and grazing grounds and was the raiding unit of the past. Members of a given clan all use the same camel *wasm*.

Clans are further sub-divided into family groupings known as *hamoula* or *fakhd*. These would generally be called lineages in English, and consist of all those people who are related within five generations: ie who have the same great-great-grandfather in the paternal line. The lineage is an important unit in a bedouin's life. It is the basis of the herding economy, for it is these families who camp together for at least part of the year, the leaders of the various lineages making up the clan council.

The tightest grouping is the kin group, the relatives through three generations. A bedouin's life was dependant on his kin, and his kin were dependant on him. Neither could fail the other and retain their honour. If a bedouin was killed, his whole kin were responsible for avenging his

78

murder. If, on the other hand, he killed someone else, every member of his kin bore the responsibility for the shedding of blood and might be killed in revenge. A man's honour could be stained by an act of one of his kin; the honour of the whole group could be forfeited by one of its members.

When violent death occurred in the desert, the kin group of the murderer might have to pack their tents and flee to the protection of some distant tribe, in the hope of escaping the vengeance which must follow them. From this distant refuge they would try to negotiate the payment of 'blood money' to the kin of the dead man. Usually, if a life had not been taken in revenge during the first few days of anger, blood money would be accepted. Blood money for killing a relative was fifty camels; for killing a man of another tribe it was seven camels. Today a blood price equivalent to about six camels (or £4,000) is levied when a man is killed in a road accident in Arabia. In former centuries the blood price acted as a check on indiscriminate killing in the desert. 'I am inclined to think that this salutary institution has contributed, in a greater degree than any other circumstance, to prevent the warlike tribes of Arabia from exterminating one another', wrote John Burckhardt in 1816.

The tribes are ruled through a remarkably democratic power structure. There is no autocratic authority in the desert, no subjection of one man to another. Decisions are taken by a series of councils with their basis in the family groups, moving up through the clan and sub-tribe councils to the main council of the tribe itself. At all levels any individual can speak up in the *majlis* (assembly) and make his opinions heard. At all levels, decisions are taken on the basis of discussion among the chosen representatives formed of the older, wiser members of the group and also the most dynamic younger ones.

The Shaikh

The paramount shaikh is chosen by the tribal council from the leading family of the tribe. Inheritance does not pass automatically from father to eldest son; often a brother of the former shaikh is chosen, or the best of his sons, or, if he has lived to be very old, perhaps his grandson may inherit his role. He is chosen for his ability, wisdom and natural powers of leadership. In the past his record as a warrior was also important, as was a certain intangible asset of being blessed with good luck.

He rules by consent and by strength of his personality and the wisdom of his judgements. If he loses the consent of his people he may be deposed. Doughty described the *majlis* of Shaikh Motlog, head of the Fuqara tribe:

> When the mejlis assembled numerous at his booth, he, the great sheykh and host, would sit out with a proud humility among the common people, holding still his looks at the ground; but they were full of unquiet sideglances, as his mind was erect and watching. His authority slumbered till, there being some just occasion, he ruled with a word the unruly Beduw . . . The sheykh of a nomad tribe is no tyrant; a great sheykh striking a tribesman he should bruise his own honour.

In the past the paramount shaikh was more important as the war leader of his tribe. Today he usually lives in the city and has become remote from the day-to-day life of his tribesmen, although his close relatives will probably stay in the desert with the tribe. The shaikh's importance nowadays lies in his ability to negotiate between his tribesmen and the governing authorities of the state in which they live. He keeps a big house and entertains his tribesmen with generous hospitality; he tries to solve their problems in the face of increasingly complex bureaucratic regulations, and to obtain for them a larger share of social services and government subsidies. Many specialists have remarked that, as a result, the shaikh is becoming more distant from his people. He no longer lives as they do; his income derives from other sources than his herds; he is recognised as the representative of his tribe, and so is accorded special treatment by the authorities. The days are gone when the shaikh's home was virtually identical to that of his tribesmen, simply one or two poles longer.

Tribal Law

The shaikhs of tribe and clan acted as judges in cases of dispute until very recently. There were also hereditary judges in the tribes who could be called on when a friendly intermediary had failed to settle a dispute. The basic principle of tribal law was that there should be reasonable compensation for the victim. Harsh punishments were not exacted against wrongdoers, but they were expected to pay compensation. Judgements were given on the basis of precedent, much as they are in British justice, and judges sought to establish ancient custom, or at least a previous example of their case.

Two witnesses of good repute were needed to establish the guilt of the accused. If a decision could not be reached, the judge might resort to trial by ordeal, such as licking a hot metal plate. It was said that in this test the innocent man would not be burned, but the tongue of the guilty would burn (possibly because his mouth was dry with nervousness).

Today tribal law has been abolished or superseded throughout the Middle East. It has been replaced by the Islamic *shari'a* law or by the secular legal system of the country concerned. Even in the past, disputes between nomadic and settled people came under state jurisdiction.

The tribes have never been totally separate from the settled communities of the lands in which they lived, and today these links are stronger than ever. All tribes have nomadic sections out in the desert and other sections living perhaps in an oasis to which the tribe lays claim, or in a desert town which is considered as the tribe's headquarters. The nomads were very dependent on their settled relatives for goods and services, and offered them protection in exchange, and grazing services in winter and spring.

Today the nomadic tribes not only have settled or semi-settled sections with whom they maintain close relations, but practically every nomadic family has one or more relatives who have left the desert and gone to settle in the city. For perhaps a generation or more these former nomads keep up their relationship with their tribal family, going out to visit them in the desert and welcoming relatives who come into the town. But gradually the ties loosen; the oil company executive or the government official or the taxi driver begins to identify with his town neighbours; he ceases to feel that, above all, he is of the Huwaytat or the Shammar or the Al Murrah.

6

ARTS AND CRAFTS

Visual arts and crafts were not, on the whole, particularly important to the bedouin in times past. The barren nature of their land and their nomadic existence, in which all belongings must be packed and repacked at frequent intervals, certainly did not encourage artistic effort involving implements and materials. Other peoples, however, living an equally deprived and nomadic existence, have produced fine visual art in the form of paintings, sculpture and carvings of one kind or another: rock carvings from ancient Arabia and the Sahara show that the desert nomads too were once interested in visual art. Just as the Old Testament had done, however, Islam decreed that its followers should not make graven images, and Muslims interpreted this as a ban on representations of human and even animal figures.

Rock-carving was a widely practised art throughout the deserts of the Middle East in pre-Islamic times, and has indeed continued in simple form right through to the present day. The earliest rock art, which cannot be precisely dated, must nevertheless have been executed thousands of years before the time of Christ, since it depicts animals (such as mammoths in the Sahara) which became extinct in the distant past. The carvings were made by hammering on a smooth rock face with a harder stone, pecking out the surface. Sometimes the rock surface was smoothed and prepared before carving began. The only indication of the age of any given carving is the amount of patina it has acquired; the darker the carvings, the older they are.

Some of the older groups of carvings show figures of people dancing,

23 Rock carvings of c 3000 BC. These show long-horned cattle which no longer exist in this part of the world. The darkness of the patina denotes the great age of the carving (*author*)

hunting, or herding animals which may no longer be kept in the deserts. Rock-carvings in Arabia, for example, show long-horned cattle which could not live in the desert there today. Attempts have been made to find the age of the carvings by comparing the dress of the people shown with examples from Egypt which could be dated to pre-dynastic or early dynastic times.

Rock-carving, though of a quite different character, reached its peak in the Arabian desert with the culture developed by the Nabataeans, the Arab tribe which established trading cities at the oasis towns of Petra and Medain Salih, in the last few centuries before Christ. These people carved rock tombs with magnificently ornate façades in the red sandstone cliffs around their towns and, as the influence of the Roman Empire spread eastwards, their rock tombs acquired more and more the

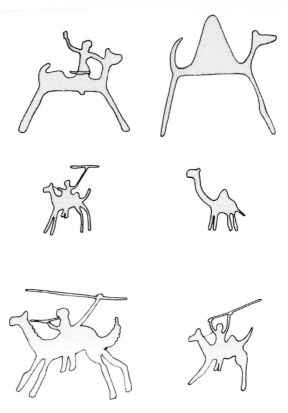

24 Ancient drawings of camels on rocks

appearance of Roman palaces. Most of the figures of people, with which they adorned their tombs, lost their heads to the puritanical bedouin in later ages.

The bedouin themselves continued to carve pictures of their animals, mostly camels, throughout the Islamic period. They also carved pictures of the other creatures who shared the deserts with them – ostrich, gazelle and oryx, and sometimes, seated on a camel, they carved the picture of a rider. These pictures have given interesting information on the way the bedouin learned to ride the camel, their early experiments on where to sit and how to saddle the animal efficiently.

A little over two thousand years ago, when the nomads were learning to make the best of their camels, the flourishing civilisations of Saba and neighbouring states in south Arabia had spread the use of literacy through much of the peninsula, and the rocks were carved with many thousands of inscriptions at a period when most of northern Europe was illiterate. Some relate the activities of kings of the day; most are simply the comments of passing caravan men who whiled away an idle hour carving a record of their presence. The only comparable carvings left by later desert dwellers are the many inscriptions of camel *wasms*.

Weaving

The most highly developed craft of the bedouin, and one which gives scope for considerable art, is an essentially practical one: weaving. The nomad's home and much of its furnishings is created by the womenfolk on their looms. On these they weave the long strips of goat-hair cloth which are sewn together to form the black tent; they weave the rather more decorative panels which form the back wall of the tent, and the still more ornate ones which make the internal dividing walls.

This decorative weaving also produces rugs on which to sit and sleep, bags for storage, saddle bags for camels and horses, and a wide variety of ornate trappings for their mounts. In this equipment for their menfolk's riding camels and mares, the women's artistic expression reaches its peak. They use a range of colours – reds, oranges, creams and browns – and produce colourful narrow strips which can be decorated with tassels and sewn together in a huge fringe, or hung separately around the animals' necks.

The patterns which are woven into these objects are largely geometric: based on stripes, squares and, especially, triangles. These are combined together to form diamond shapes, or one triangle may be inverted above another. The colours came, in the past, from natural dyes extracted from desert plants; nowadays the wool is often artificially dyed in the towns and the colours are brighter and rather more garish.

The wool is plucked or shorn from the family's sheep and goats. The goat hair, which is frequently black, is stronger and more waterproof,

25 A leather bag for storing coffee beans, decorated with a woven silk panel and tassels (*author*)

and is therefore normally used for the roofs of tents, whereas it may be mixed with wool for side walls and bags. The women tease out the wool and hair by hand, comb it with a wooden board set with nails, then spin it on a spindle looking like a wooden cross with a hook at the top. They may walk about tending their flocks and spinning the spindle between their hands, or they may sit or stand and spin it against their thighs. In western Arabia the wool is sometimes held in a cleft stick, a distaff, which is tucked under the woman's arm and from which it is spun onto the spindle.

The thread is then wound off the spindle into a ball and is ready for weaving. This the bedouin women do on a ground loom. The loom

26 A face mask, decorated with coins and buttons, worn by bedouin women of western Arabia (*author*)

consists simply of a few bars of wood which can easily be transported. When the woman is ready to weave she attaches the warp threads to rods which are tied to the two beams, and these are then pegged down to the ground. Between the beams the threads are gathered over a central rod, the heddle, which is held up above the threads by being lodged on a stone, a piece of wood or a can. A shed stick is inserted between the threads on one side, and a wooden beater on the other.

The thread to be woven is wound around a stick spool which acts as a shuttle; this is passed between the raised threads and forced into place with the beater and with little picks made of gazelle horns. A detailed description of the whole weaving process is given by Shelagh Weir who emphasises how hard this work is, and how much the finished product depends on the women's physical strength as well as skill.

The women sit on the ground to weave their cloth, and, later, as they progress along the loom they sit on the woven material itself. The loom is not very wide (usually only about 60–90cm, 2–3ft) but the strips of cloth are then sewn together to make wider tent sections or rugs. Sometimes two women work together on the same strip of material.

The women of goat- and sheep-rearing tribes weave more than those of the camel tribes, who do not have the wool to hand and are more often on the move. The camel herders may buy the woven cloth which they need in the *souqs* of the desert market towns, which sell strips of all weights and dimensions, made both by other bedouin and by weavers in the towns. The women of shepherd tribes living near these market towns spend much of their day weaving since they have a ready and profitable market for their wares. They seem, at present, to like to produce a variety of goods, rather than to specialise in a single item.

Leather Work

Leather work is another field in which the women have the chance to create decorative objects. Traditionally they have used the skins of animals as bags for storing coffee beans, dates and other food, as well as for water-skins. The hides are treated with salt, then a tanning mixture made from roots, bark and desert plants, then rubbed with fat or camel marrow. The smaller bags are decorated with burnt patterns (now often drawn on with a ball-point pen), long leather fringes, and also with some leather appliqué work and cowrie shells. Today the women have extended this decoration, especially on their coffee bags, to include woven sections and tassels made of silk bought in the towns, small silver and glass beads sewn onto the appliquéd sections, and bits of coloured material of one sort or another. Plaited leather thongs are used to close the necks of the bags, and to hang them on the tent walls.

Home-treated leather was also used for babies' cradles, buckets, and camel troughs, as well as for storage bags. Bedouin babies are still kept in

27 Woman in western Arabia winding off wool, which she has just spun, from her spindle to the ball at her feet

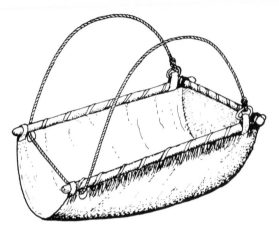

28 A baby's leather cradle which can be hung from his mother's shoulder or
from the tent pole. The cradle has three wooden struts to hold the sides and
head end rigid. It closes across the baby's feet when suspended by the
leather cords

such little cradles, carried around on their mothers' shoulders or hung
from a hook on the tent pole, out of reach of scorpions and harmful
insects. The cradle is made of an oblong of leather sewn onto wooden
bars on three sides, with a drawn thong at each end. When the baby is
placed inside and the cradle suspended, the thong at the foot end closes
the bag, keeping the baby firmly inside, while the bar across the head

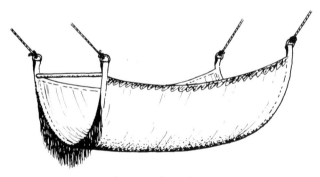

29 Bedouin cradle made of camel hide

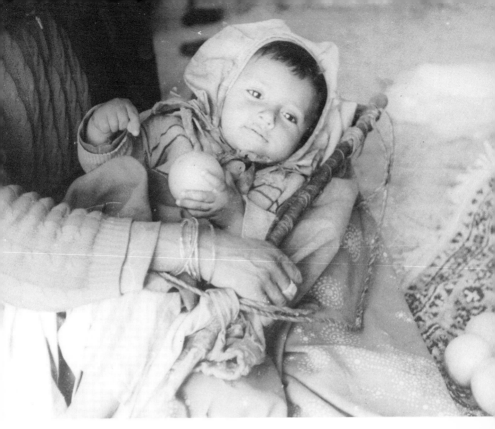

30 Bedouin baby being placed in his leather cradle which would then be hung from a hook on the tent pole (*author*)

end ensures that the bag does not crush its skull.

Large water-bags, buckets and troughs are today often made of car tyres and inner tubes rather than of leather, and the scope, or perhaps the urge, for decorating has not been extended to this material.

The men, too, enjoyed decorating, or having decorated, the objects which they used daily. Their rifles were often ornamented with sheet silver or other metals, and sometimes they decorated the butt with gazelle or oryx teeth. They also padded it with gazelle skin, perhaps as much for comfort, to soften the kick, as for ornament. Wooden milking-bowls, platters, and pestles for grinding coffee were studded with tiny metal nails, forming geometric silvery patterns, or brass studs. Their

place has often been taken today by brightly coloured, imported, enamelled pots, pans and trays.

Bedouin Silver

It is in the field of jewellery and silverwork that men and women have
had the greatest opportunity to indulge in personal decoration. The
bedouin did not make the jewellery or silverware which they used
themselves, but they provided a large market for it and helped deter-
mine the styles.

Men's ornamentation came in the practical form of daggers, long
knives, swords, and powder and cartridge belts. The most ornate of
these was the small curved dagger, the *khanjar*, worn at the front of
the belt. While the dagger itself was a simple functional object, its
sheath was plated with silver, engraved, chased, embossed, or otherwise decorated with studs or finely plaited silver threads or cords. The
intricate workmanship of some of these sheaths is in sharp contrast to
the simplicity of most bedouin decoration.

Bedouin jewellery was made largely of rather poor quality silver.
The main source of silver in the little desert towns where it was produced was the Maria Theresa dollar, the coin (originally Austrian)
which continued to be produced in London for a century or so after it
dropped out of currency in Europe. The silver from these coins was
mixed with other metals, most commonly with copper.

Much of the bedouin jewellery is heavy and crudely worked, but
there are also some fine pieces showing considerable skill in their
technique. The arts of filigree and granulation (soldering small drops
onto a silver base) were always popular and effective; some of the semi-
precious stones used, coral and amber especially in the west, turquoise
(from Iran) in the east, look very attractive in their rough settings. The
bedouin were not fussy, however, and an odd mixture of glass beads and
shells was equally attractive to them. I have a simple necklace of glass
beads and cowrie shells, bought in the *souq* of Damascus. I have twice
had to excuse myself (on the grounds that it was a present from my little
daughter) for not offering it to women who fingered it admiringly and

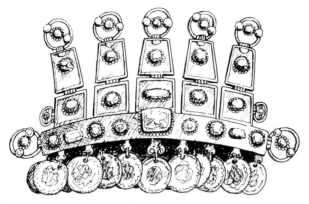

31 Part of a woman's headdress

covetously. One of these bedouin women pointed out the cowrie shells and said without hesitation 'It must be from our people'; Damascus was over a thousand miles away from her tent.

Jewellery is especially worn at weddings and the bride may be so weighed down with heavy necklaces, collars, anklets, bracelets and

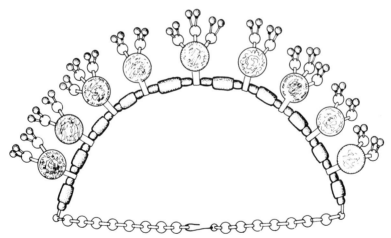

32 A typical bedouin necklace which combines amber and other beads with silver coins and simple silver ornamentation

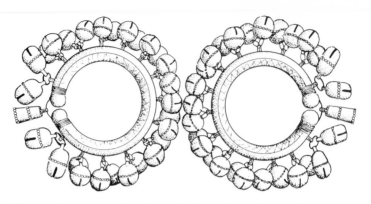

33 Silver anklets decorated with small silver bells. Such jewellery was worn especially for wedding celebrations; individual pieces are often quite heavy

ornate headpieces that she can scarcely move. The jewellery may be part of her dowry, or come as a wedding gift from her husband as part of the bride price; in either case it remains her personal property come what may. Some women literally wear their wealth round their necks, in the shape of coin necklaces, or – in western Arabia – on their masque-like veils which are sometimes thickly encrusted with coins.

Particularly popular are little silver boxes and phials in which a verse of the Koran can be kept as a protection against evil. These are hung round the neck and come in many shapes and sizes. Other talismans against ill fortune are also worn, especially blue beads to ward off the 'evil eye' which are often sewn onto a baby's cap.

Music

The bedouin traditionally made one or two simple musical instruments which they used to accompany singing, reciting or dancing, usually around the camp fires at night. The instruments were made in the same basic fashion, although the end result was quite different.

Two kinds of instruments are used: stringed instruments and drums or tambourines. Both are made by stretching an animal skin over a wooden

34 An ornamented amulet of a kind very popular with the bedouin. A written verse of the Koran, or a charm, could be placed inside the amulet to ward off evil

35 Part of a silver headdress of a kind worn for ceremonial occasions, especially by a bride

frame; this is then tightened before use, by heating in front of the fire. The stringed instrument, the *rababah*, is a simple lute with one string. It has a flat, oblong, sounding board and is played with a simple bow to produce a rather wailing note.

Musical instruments fell out of favour in Arabia under the puritanical Wahhabi revival, but nowadays are generally accepted and enjoyed again, although the lute is not usually played by pure bedouin but by servants and lesser tribes.

Poetry

Undoubtedly the bedouin's greatest and noblest artistic achievement, and the one closest to their hearts, is their poetry. It is the perfect vehicle for self-expression and artistic creation in the limited environment of the tent since it requires no equipment, or materials, nothing but the natural skill of the poet and the lively memory of his listeners. This poetry was not written down in the desert, but has been transmitted orally over the centuries; the best poems from the pre-Islamic period were preserved in this way and are still remembered today.

No one knows when poetry was first developed by the desert nomads. The earliest bedouin poems surviving now date from about AD 500 and are already in a highly developed, polished form. Little has been added in fact to the poetic forms perfected in pre-Islamic times; they are still the 'classics', supreme examples of Arabic verse.

Bedouin poetry is essentially limited in its themes, just as the scope of bedouin life is limited. Favourite subjects are love and war; essential episodes include the nostalgia of an abandoned camp site, the qualities and virtues of the camel and horse, the arts of hospitality. Many poems ended with a song of praise to some great man from whom the poet was hoping to receive suitable patronage.

Although the subjects of the poems are limited, the language in which they are recited is extraordinarily rich and the verses are crowded with imagery. Simile is piled on simile, comparisons being drawn with the delicately beautiful wild creatures of the desert, the brilliance of the night sky, the noble refinement of the Arabian horse. The art of the poet lies here, in the richness of the language with which he can adorn an old theme; there is no call on him to find new subjects to recount. His listeners are satisfied with the old and well worn.

An excellent introduction to bedouin poetry is provided by William Polk in his translation and interpretation of *The Golden Ode* by Labid Ibn Rabiah, one of the last of the great pre-Islamic poets (a second edition of this work has now been published by the American University in Cairo). While preparing his translation Polk travelled with the bedouin by camel across the Nefud desert in Arabia and he used this experience to interpret the poem. He also used photographs of bedouin life to illustrate each page of verse.

The poem opens in typical fashion, the poet's memory of an old love stirred by his coming upon a long-abandoned camp site:

> Effaced are the camp sites, both the stopping points and the camping grounds
> In Minan [central Najd] both Ghaul and Rijam have become the haunts of wild beasts.
> And the flood channels of Ar-Raiyan, their traces are stripped away,
> Worn smooth, just like writings on rocks.
> Dung, no longer renewed after a period of frequenting the site . . .
> Nay, do not think longer of the girl Nawar since she has gone far away;
> And her ties and bindings to you are sundered.
> A woman of the people of Muriyah who briefly camped at Faid and then became a neighbour
> To the people of the Hijaz. So where can longing for her get you? . . .

The form in which these poems is written is the ode, called *qasida* in Arabic. It consists of some 20–100 couplets; the same rhyme is maintained throughout the whole length of the poem. In Arabic it is less difficult than it may sound to find 200 rhyming words, since there are only three vowels, many words have standard feminine endings, and pronouns are attached to the ends of nouns (the pronoun *hā*, meaning it, its, her, hers, formed the last part of the rhyme in the poem above). However, the rhyme involves the last two or three syllables in every line (three in the above case) and the skill needed to build such lengthy rhymes into the poem, so that they appear to occur naturally, is of the highest order.

The metres used in these odes are thought to correspond to the walking pace of the camel or the horse, indicating that the poems may have been composed during the long treks across the desert, when the poet was jogging along in solitude above his camel's hump. Professor Arberry, whose translations of Arabic poetry provide a more comprehensive introduction to the subject, maintains that it is more likely that the rhythms were inspired by the beating of drums.

The Professor gives a translation of a war poem which could well have found a suitable accompaniment in drumming. It is attributed to the sixth-century warrior poet, Antara Ibn Shaddad, son of an Arab father and an Abyssinian mother, the 'Black Knight' who became the hero of so extensive an Arab folklore that his figure is still often portrayed today. His poem runs:

> I have a high purpose firmer than a rock and stronger than immovable mountains,
> And a sword which, when I strike with it ever, the useless spearheads give way before it,
> And a lance point which, whenever I lose my way in the night, guides me and restores me from straying,
> And a mettlesome steed that never sped, but that the lightning trailed behind it from the striking of its hooves.
> Dark of hue [it is], splitting the starless night with a blackness, between its eyes a blaze like the crescent moon,
> Ransoming me with its own life, and I ransom it with my life, on the day of the battle, and [with] my wealth.
> And whenever the market of the war of the tall lances is afoot, and it blazes with the polished, whetted blades,
> I am the broker thereof, and my spearpoint is a merchant purchasing precious souls.
> Wild beasts of the wilderness, when war breaks into flame, follow me from the empty wastes;
> Follow me, [and] you will see the blood of the foemen streaming between the hillocks and the sands . . .

The rhyme and the rhythm of Arabic poetry can rarely be conveyed in translation, so that much of the pleasure of its immensely rich language is lost to the foreigner; but it is nevertheless extremely evocative of the atmosphere of desert life.

Present-day bedouin poems tell of love and war, gatherings around the coffee hearth, and tiring journeyings, just as those of the past did. They are recited, or chanted to musical accompaniment, while sitting in the still of the evening around the camp fire. A favourite game among the verbally talented bedouin is for one person to make up a line of poetry, and for the next to produce a following line, and so on around the circle, each contributor keeping to the rhythm and rhyme scheme set in the first line.

Many recent poems have been collected and translated by modern travellers and can be found in the major studies of the bedouin. Specialised collections are not available.

7

THE LIFE LOST

The Heroic Age

Bedouin poetry and story-telling reverted again and again to the matter closest to their hearts, the subject of their dreams, the proof of their manhood: war in the desert. Until quite recently, within living memory, the desert was never at peace, never still. Raids and counter-raids, flaring occasionally into genuine tribal warfare, swept to and fro, keeping every tribe on the alert, every male permanently on his toes.

For the bedouin, raiding and fighting were not only the occupations which he took most seriously and to which he devoted most care, attention and sacrifice; they were also his favourite sport, the pastime for which he lived. Colonel Dickson, who camped frequently with the bedouin of Kuwait between 1929 and 1936, wrote that 'raiding is the breath of life' to the bedouin who would become 'the most melancholy of men' without it. But Dickson was witnessing the twilight of a way of life which has vanished from the desert, probably for ever.

Bedouin fighting was no haphazard affair: it was conducted according to a set of rules every bit as rigid as those of medieval chivalry – which the Arab example may have strongly influenced. To break these rules would bring such shame and dishonour on a man or his tribe that it was rarely contemplated; to succeed while abiding by the strictest and most difficult regulations would cover an individual and his tribe with honour and glory, the most coveted good in the bedouin world.

The basis of the bedouin code was fair play. One fought only those who could fight back: women and children must not be touched (only Turks, westerners and city dwellers were barbaric enough to risk harming them), nor must a guest in one's tents (however unwelcome), nor an unarmed shepherd boy. Raiders aimed to launch a surprise attack on the victim's herds and camp, but it would have been most shameful to make it a real surprise by attacking between the hours of midnight and sunrise when the defenders would be asleep. When a man sleeps, the bedouin say, his soul leaves the body through the nostrils and wanders about. At such times an evil spirit may enter the sleeping man and take possession of him, and he will wake as one who is mad. Because a sleeping person has no soul it is as though he were dead, and so it is forbidden to kill a sleeping man, even in a blood feud.

It was far more honourable to attack at sunrise, when the defenders had all day to try to recover their lost herds, than at sunset when the raiders could more easily fade away into the dark. War (and raids) could only be engaged after a proper declaration of hostilities; a surprise attack on a tribe with whom one was at peace would blacken the honour of the attacker.

While the bedouin's life is so harsh that they grow up relatively indifferent to suffering and death, they would not spill blood wantonly in their fighting. The blood price was a check on indiscriminate killing, and the code of honour forbade harming or killing wounded enemies at the mercy of the victors. Wounded comrades were carried to safety if there was any possibility of doing so. Honour in battle did not demand a stand to the finish either. It was a case of 'he who fights and runs away lives to fight another day' for the bedouin who saw the odds stacked against him; in such a case he would judge it folly, not heroism, to stay and be killed. But if the odds were even, he would fight ferociously and stoically.

The aim of a raid, then, was loot rather than killing. Yet even this must be sacrificed when the code demanded it. The women and children of a defeated enemy must not be left unprovided for. To each woman was given one of the stolen camels on which she and her children could make their way to the camp of their nearest relatives. And a camel so given became the woman's own, inalienable property. Noble raiders could even sometimes be persuaded to return stolen camels or horses to their male owners when it was shown that in some way their 'lifting' had not been quite fair play.

Carl Raswan, who lived for years with the bedouin before and after World War I and became involved in their raiding and warfare, estimated that without their strict code of honour 'all human life in nomad Arabia would have become extinct long since'. He said this with feeling, after saving his own life and that of his companions by obtaining a cup of coffee (which classed them as guests) in an enemy tent to which they had gone for peace negotiations.

Raiding

When the hot dead days of summer were over and the bedouin were able to move about the desert again, the men would begin to dream of and plan a *ghazu*, a raid destined to carry off the camel herds and horses of a hostile tribe. There was nothing reprehensible in such an activity in their eyes; on the contrary, they were confident of divine backing: 'We raid because we're bedouin and the bedu have Allah's permission to devour their neighbours herds', one of the Fuqara tribe told Fathers Jaussen and Savignac who visited them in 1909.

Raiding for the bedouin was an alternative to trading, and far more fun. While camels were the basis of the bedouin economy, and this basis was highly vulnerable to drought or sickness, they were not, in practice, bought and sold between tribes. Within a tribe, ups and downs of fortune in camel breeding would be remedied by gifts or levies from the fortunate; between tribes, the only way of repairing losses was to raid the herds of a luckier tribe. Another year, when the rains had changed or fortune swung the other way, they would raid back in return.

In the desert, raiding was a man's chief hope of advancement, perhaps the only way in which he could better his lot. In the Sahara, as Lloyd Cabot Briggs noted, raiding on a major scale was one of the most important elements of the economy, and was run almost as a formalised industry before the French put a stop to it.

The raid would be planned in an atmosphere of excited anticipation and secrecy. Surprise was the essence of success and there were always a few strangers staying in a camp who might spread an incautious word. The key figure in any raid was the leader, the *aqid* (a term now used for 'colonel' in modern Arab armies). He would plan the strategy and direct the operation as well as supervising distribution of the booty afterwards. It was most important to find an *aqid* who was not only capable and courageous, but also known for his good luck.

The active able-bodied men of the camp were all eligible to take part, and boys from the age of about twelve or so might hope to be given a chance to 'win their spurs'. Young boys were most likely to be included in the spring raids, when the going would be less hard as the desert would provide ample grazing for their camels on the long trek home. Spring was the favourite season for raiding, since it gave the highest chance of bringing stolen herds back alive and healthy. Summer raids were far more gruelling, although the enemy, camped close to his wells, was most vulnerable at that time. For summer raids only men in their prime, between the ages of sixteen and forty, were usually considered.

A young boy returning successfully from his first raid would try to sacrifice a sheep or goat, to offer thanks for his fortune and ensure success in the future. Perhaps the youngest raider recorded was a little Rwala boy who, unannounced and uninvited, accompanied a raid in which Carl Raswan took part. When the raiders camped on their first night out after twelve hours' hard riding, they found curled up asleep in one of their camel bags, eight year old Emir Fuaz, (grandson of paramount Shaikh Nuri Ibn Shaalan), a wild little creature who grew up to become leader of the Rwala. He begged to be allowed to stay with the raid and, after a two month's expedition, was allotted four camels as his share of the booty.

Raids could, and often did, extend over very long distances and hence lasted many months. Raids up to 800km (500 miles) away were quite common in Arabia; even greater distances (round trips of 1,500 miles or so) were covered in the Sahara. The advantage of picking a distant tribe as one's victim was the difficulty which that tribe would have in retaliating later. Raids on one's own doorstep (so to speak) could bring too rapid retribution.

As the raiding party might number anything from twenty to several hundreds, careful preparation of supplies and route were essential. The raiders would journey out on their riding camels, while those who owned a mare led her alongside. The mares would be used in the attack, for which they were faster than camels, but had not the stamina to be ridden on the long trek to and from the raid. Mares could not be taken further than about 100 miles from home, or where supplies of water were not reasonably assured. Each man would also carry a supply of dates and flour, his own water skin and, of course, his rifle and ammunition.

They might leave the camp heading in a direction quite different from the one they must eventually pursue, and only once out in the wilderness would the rank and file of raiders be told their destination. Along with the leader would travel the seer. It was considered most important to interpret correctly favourable and unfavourable signs along the way and important moves must be made on lucky rather than unlucky days. They would set out on a Monday or a Thursday, but never fight on the 6th, 16th or 21st of any month. If the leader was at a loss what to do he might take the advice of the seer.

Scouts would go out ahead of the raiding party to check the position and movements of the enemy herds. When the raid was to be launched the raiders would divide into two parties, one to drive off the herds, the other to lie in ambush to cut off the enemy horsemen when they came pouring out of their camp. This group would take the brunt of the fighting. If they won, the whole band of raiders would set off to drive the stolen herds home. If they lost, the enemy would recover their herds and the raiders would save their skins as best they could.

The first few days of the retreat were tense and required long marches. The raiders might take a zigzag course to try to throw off pursuit; they might leave a rearguard to hold any passes on their route. They would seek difficult ground away from any camps for it was not at all unknown for a successful raiding party to loose their booty to other raiders on the way home.

Once the successful raiders reached their tents the booty was instantly divided. Any man who had taken a mare kept it. The leader would take first choice of the camels captured, then any who had distinguished themselves particularly would choose, and so on according to the role a man had played. Or the camels might be allotted by chance – the leader might take a halter from each raider, walk along the line of camels and place a halter on each beast, at which the raiders would claim that wearing their own halter. A fine she-camel would be sacrificed in thanks for success.

A noble leader might claim almost no booty for himself. Father Jaussen records that in a raid in which the Fuqara followed Audah Abu Tayah, paramount shaikh of the Huwaytat, Audah claimed only five of the 400 camels taken.

This Audah is best known to us of any desert fighter. He lived at a time when adventurous Europeans were beginning to penetrate the deserts and recount their experiences there, but when the bedouin were still masters in their own environment, raiding and fighting to their hearts' content. To Musil, who met him in 1909, he was reported as having eaten the hearts of fallen enemies 'on several occasions'.

Audah, in the words of T.E. Lawrence (Lawrence of Arabia) was 'the greatest fighting man in northern Arabia'. He had to be won to the Arab cause and, early in 1917, Lawrence met the tough old man (then over fifty) and his eleven year old son Muhammad. Lawrence conjures Audah from the page with the skill of a magician.

> A tall strong figure with a haggard face, passionate and tragic . . . He had large eloquent eyes like black velvet in richness. His forehead was low and broad, his nose very high and sharp, powerfully hooked: his mouth rather large and mobile . . . His generosity kept him always poor despite the profits of a hundred raids . . . [but] . . . he was careful to be at enmity with nearly all the tribes in the desert, that he might have proper scope for raids.

Audah's adventures with Lawrence during the Arab revolt in the desert, of which he was the backbone, in no way sated his passion for raiding which he continued into old age. The story of a disastrous raid recounted later by Audah's son Muhammad to another Briton, Sir Alec Kirkbride (and related by him in *A Crackle of Thorns*), is a telling example of the hazards which all raiders faced.

36 A great desert warrior of the first quarter of the twentieth century, Audah Abu Tayah of the Huwaytat (*Middle East Centre, Oxford*)

Muhammad told how, in 1921, a raid was planned with Audah as the leader, and some 120 men gathered in the desert east of Ma'an in southern Jordan. Their goal was the herds of Iraqi tribes, grazing on the west bank of the Euphrates, north west of Baghdad some 640km (400

106

miles) away. When they approached their destination they were spotted by a single rider, probably an enemy scout, whom they could not overtake. Now the enemy would know of their coming, the element of surprise was lost and they must abandon the raid which would be doomed to failure.

They turned for home but the first essential was to replenish their water skins, to take them across the intervening desert. They made for wells near Rutbah. As they approached they saw troops with armoured cars at the wells and, fearing these were Iraqi authorities out to capture them, they fled into the desert. Only afterwards was it known that the troops were in fact a group of British RAF men who would have taken no interest in the bedouin warriors.

The next waterhole, 210km (125 miles) to the west, was found to be dry. The raiders were now at the end of their tether; they rounded on Audah blaming him for their failure and broke up into small groups, each going its own way, after sharing out the remaining dregs of water. Twenty-five Huwaytat followed Audah in a nightmare forced march, moving in long night stages and halting over midday. When a camel died they opened its stomach to drink the liquid there. Its rider doubled up on another camel until there were no more seats available, for no starving camel could carry more than two men. Then the owner of any camel that died was left behind to face certain death in the desert.

Young Muhammad finished his last drop of water and rode on for twenty-four hours under the scorching sun without any further liquid. He began to faint and whispered to his father to go on without him, he could continue no more. Audah murmured through cracked and bleeding lips: 'Try to hold on till nightfall.' That night the old man pulled out a hidden water bottle and both took a small mouthful. The wily old man's secret store saved him and his son and enabled them to reach home, along with six of their companions. The other members of the raiding party had fared no better. Of the 120 men who had set out, over ninety did not return. They had perished in the desert.

This story of Audah and his son is more telling, because of its pointless tragedy, than the far greater number of exultant tales of successful raids. It is also perhaps more significant, for raiding, which had for the bedouin the compulsive attraction of gambling, inevitably also involved a net loss. True, a strong tribe could grow stronger by taking others' herds, but more often than not herds taken would be lost again in a counter-raid, or stolen by a third party. The total number of camels declined through losses en route and sacrifices, and the loss of men was even more absolute.

'Their ghrazzus and counter-ghrazzus are the destruction of the Aarab' wrote Charles Doughty in the 1870s. When all the excitement is over 'in the end it is but an ill exchange of cattle'. He noted that the herds of his hosts, the Fuqara, were ill balanced because not home-bred but robbed from several different *diras*.

Tribal Wars

More serious fighting arose in tribal warfare when whole tribes, or federations of tribes, took the field against each other. These wars are well documented for northern Arabia in the last few decades of the last century and the first few of this, and are particularly interesting since out of them grew the present day state of Saudi Arabia.

At the beginning of this century three city states based on tribal powers were struggling for supremacy, aided or hindered by other strong tribes whose allegiance was not firmly cast. The three dynasties were those of Ibn Rashid of Hail, supported by the Shammar tribe, the Ibn Saud of Riyadh, supported by the Anazah confederation, and the Ashraf of Mecca (the Hashemites), supported by the tribes of the Hejaz.

Their struggles were practically the last convulsions of true bedouin warfare and one of their battles was particularly noted in the west because a young Englishman died in it. His name was Captain Shakespear and he had accompanied his friend Abd al Aziz Ibn Saud in an attack on the Ibn Rashid in 1915. Abd al Aziz was supported by some 6,000 enlisted townsmen and bedouin, and thousands of allied tribesmen. His opponent's army consisted of some 700 Hail townsmen and 8–9,000 Shammar bedouin. The armies clashed at Jarab and initially Ibn Saud appeared to be carrying the day. But when things went against the Ajman tribe, who were in his lines, they defected and the battle was lost. In the rout Shakespear was shot.

37 A silver powder casket which was worn on the warrior's wide belt. It is ornamented with religious inscriptions (*author*)

Tribal war was by that stage becoming a serious affair, due to the
large number of guns which were finding their way into the desert.
Only a few years before it had retained more of the atmosphere of
medieval conflict than of modern battle.

Rules had to be observed, as with raiding, and there could be no fighting without a formal declaration of hostilities. A pre-emptive surprise
attack would have been totally dishonourable (and perhaps it was this
tribal memory which caused the deep Arab indignation over the Israeli
pre-emptive attack in the 1967 war).

Before the two battle-lines clashed, outstanding heroes on one side or
the other would issue challenges to individual combat and these combats
would take place, the fight always being to the finish (exactly as in the
days of the Greeks), while the armies looked on.

Each tribe had its own battle cry, to spur its young men to courage on
the field and to enable them to identify one another in a mêlée in which

friend and foe were dressed identically. Another device to spur them to courage was the presence of a 'war queen', a custom which was only abandoned in the early part of this century, when the increased fire-power made it too dangerous.

The 'queen' was chosen from the prettiest girls of the tribe and would ride, mounted on a splendidly decked camel litter, into the heart of the battle. There she would exhort her young men in fiery words, letting down her hair and baring her breasts; it was terrible shame to her war-riors if the girl and her litter should ever be captured.

The great Rwala tribe had a very special litter for this purpose known as Abu Duhur. It was the 'ark' of their tribe, a sacred object by which (through the movement of its decorative ostrich plumes) they prophe-sied success or failure. It had been captured from the Amarat in 1793 by a Rwala fighting with the Wuld Ali. He had died in the fight and the litter had been presented to the Rwala who had held it through strength ever since.

Carl Raswan had the rare chance to witness its use when the Rwala were facing extinction in a severe drought; the whole tribe were on the move, forced north into hostile territory, their herds and children dying daily. To encourage the starving nation, surrounded by well fed enemies, a beautiful young girl was chosen to ride in Abu Duhur at their head, and to lead them on into fertile but dangerous lands. On this occasion they were fortunate; war was avoided through negotiation, and the Rwala brought their herds safely to the good grazing.

By 1930 desert warfare had become quite terrible and other factors, such as armoured cars and aeroplanes, had greatly altered its character. Colonel Dickson tells of the last bedouin wars, between Abd al Aziz Ibn Saud, by then master of Arabia, and the fanatical *Ikhwan* (Muslim Brothers) who had helped him to victory.

In 1929–30 the Ikhwan, led by Faisal al Dawlish, paramount shaikh of the Mutayr, were rebelling against their master who was now king in Riyadh. Faisal sent his oldest and favourite son, Azaiyiz, on a massive raid across northern Arabia, to convince the great tribes there that the *Ikhwan* were the power to back.

The young man, aged twenty-five, left with 650 picked camel riders and took a huge amount of booty. But on his return, he learned that the King's governor of Hail had seized and fortified vital wells on his route home. It was mid-summer and the camels were dying for lack of water. He and his comrades knew they could not go much longer without replenishing their supplies.

The older men in the raiding party advised changing route and making a long detour to the north, to avoid the enemy. Young Azaiyiz disagreed and proposed storming the enemy positions, for God was on the side of the *Ikhwan* and it would be dishonourable to avoid battle. The older men, fearful of the rash folly of this course, set off to the north, followed by 150 men and many stolen camels.

Azaiyiz and his 500 followers drew near the wells which were defended by 1,500 men of enemy tribes, all well watered and with fresh camels. Azaiyiz's force had not drunk a drop of water for eight hours, their camels were dying and the men half crazed with thirst. They stormed the defenders at noon, and for a while their fanatical courage almost carried the day against overwhelming odds. A shimmering mirage also prevented the defenders shooting accurately at a distance.

Eventually, however, numbers prevailed and, as the sun went down, forty survivors of Azaiyiz's force escaped into the desert and hid. The following day they were forced to return to the wells, unable to survive without water. A rearguard, left there, disarmed them, then went on to join the main force. When the latter heard that forty *Ikhwan* were still alive, unarmed, at the wells, they sent back a small force to shoot them all. But meanwhile, one armed *Ikhwan* had joined his fellows. When the small enemy force came back and began to shoot the unarmed men he drew his gun and shot the enemy in the backs. The remaining enemy fled and the *Ikhwan* were left with one camel and four water skins. With these slim provisions, essential for survival in the desert, they were able to make good their escape.

The battle had cost the *Ikhwan* 460 men and their opponents over 500. A thousand men fallen in one day was a high toll by bedouin standards but symptomatic of modern warfare. The loss of his favourite son is thought to have broken the spirit of Faisal al Dawish and hastened the end of the *Ikhwan* rebellion. But Azaiyiz's gallant sacrifice gained him great posthumous glory among the bedouin; as a token of his admiration for his fallen opponent, the king, once the rebellion was over, took both Azaiyiz's widows as his own wives.

Bedouin Weapons

Until the beginning of this century the bedouin were armed largely with traditional weapons which necessitated hand to hand combat, and enabled highly selective fighting and killing. The favourite weapon was the lance, consisting of an iron tip mounted on a bamboo shaft about twice the length of the horse. This lance gave a camel rider, seated high above ground on a firm saddle atop the camel's hump, a great advantage over anyone on foot.

The rise of bedouin military power in the desert coincides with the development, about the second century BC, of the firm camel saddle (called

38 Ornate silver sheath for a rather long *khanjar*. Granulation (the application of drops of silver onto a silver base) is the main technique used in its decoration

shadād from the Arabic word *shadid* meaning firm or strong) which enabled the rider to wield a long lance or sword, instead of the small bow formerly used. Its effect can be compared with the introduction of the stirrup which brought shock combat to European warfare and gave an initial advantage to the French (noticeable at the battle of Hastings) who adopted the new techniques early.

Swords were the other major weapon of attack. Their blades were forged by the local blacksmiths, the Sana, or (in North Africa at any rate) imported from Europe. Briggs recorded that many of the Tuareg swords had sixteenth- and seventeenth-century blades of Spanish or German workmanship. Raswan was presented with an historic bedouin sword said to have been made from pieces of a meteorite which destroyed a bedouin camp in the twelfth century. Small curved daggers, the *khanjar*, were, and still are, very popular. Straighter short, narrow daggers and broad long ones were also used.

Some protection against these weapons was afforded by vests of chain mail. Burckhardt recorded, in 1816, that long ones to the knees and short ones to the waist were still used in the desert. The Rwala tribe at the time owned some 200 coats of mail, made of interwoven links. Hide shields were used by foot soldiers in the Sahara and Arabia. They were made of ox-hide or dugong-skin (a large sea creature, origin of the mermaid legend) and were about 45cm (18in) in diameter.

By the latter part of the last century, a few alien weapons had found their way into the desert. Matchlock rifles were owned by some of the townsmen and the desert shaikhs in Doughty's day, but their effectiveness was limited. They could not be reloaded on horseback and a few drops of rain would quench them. Doughty tells of a battle between the bedouin and the townsmen of Anaiza in which the latter were having things all their own way, thanks to possession of 200 matchlocks, when a shower of rain drenched the matchlocks and the townsmen, who had ventured too far from their walls, were completely routed. A few of the bedouin had also acquired old, flint horse-pistols 'abandoned in our grandsires' time and sold away from Europe' as Doughty remarked.

In the early years of this century, rifles came into Arabia, especially through a trade in surplus arms which passed through Muscat after the

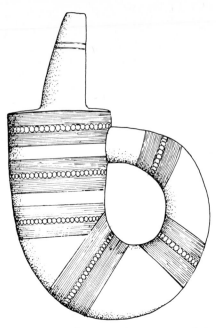

39 A decorative silver powder horn, usually worn on a belt running from the waist across one shoulder

end of the Boer War. Musil tells of an armaments caravan of 210 camels carrying over 1,000 rifles and ammunition, visiting the Rwala while he was there. It was not until World War I, however, that rifles became widespread and readily available to the bedouin who began to call all firearms 'Mausers'. From that time the bedouin have shown themselves adaptable in their use of weapons, taking happily to armed cars for raiding in the 1920s and manipulating, in today's armies, the most sophisticated of modern hardware.

It was, in the past, a generally accepted view that bedouin warfare cost few lives. Palgrave, who travelled in Arabia in the last century, wrote: 'Their feuds are continual but at little cost of life ... the bedouin ... has at heart little inclination for killing or being killed.' And Doughty, telling of a battle in which 200 men were said to have been killed, noted that one must halve the number of alleged bedouin losses to get anything like an accurate figure.

By the second and third decades of this century, however, the inevitable results of increased firepower were beginning to be felt. Although the bedouin were, according to Glubb Pasha, 'on the whole bad shots', they fought at such close range that they succeeded in inflicting casualties all the same. An early indication of the cost of desert fighting is given by Fathers Jaussen and Savignac, commenting that the Shaikh of the Fuqara had had over twenty wives but only two sons survived, thirteen having died – nearly all of them in raids or warfare.

Lawrence, ten years later, tells a more terrible tale. Audah's Abu Tayah of the Huwaytat were the best fighting men of the desert, but in thirteen years their numbers had been reduced, through death in battle, from 1,200 men to less than 500. Audah himself had slain seventy-five Arabs in battle and a countless number of Turks. Finally Musil, a few years later, remarked that, of the Rwala, four-fifths of the men died in battle or as a result of wounds received there.

It seems then that the bedouin may have been saved in the nick of time from exterminating themselves. Their centuries-old methods of warfare were revolutionised by the introduction of modern firepower early this century, bringing lethal weapons into an environment which provided no natural cover. Modern armies have found that, without air cover, in the desert they are sitting ducks. A bedouin warrior on horse or camel-back was as vulnerable to an enemy with a gun as his fellow desert dwellers, the gazelle, ostrich and oryx which have all become extinct, or virtually so, in the past few decades.

8

HOW POWER AND
LIBERTY WERE LOST

In the Sahara

The Tuareg, veiled nomadic herders of the Sahara, were the first to feel their wings clipped by the incursions of foreigners into their deserts. After hundreds of years of autonomy in the inaccessible inner reaches of the great Sahara desert, these fierce tribesmen had developed a social system at the head of which was a noble warrior class whose sole occupation was warfare. Menial tasks of everyday life were left to vassal tribesmen or negro slaves brought from south of the Sahara.

During the nineteenth century individual European explorers began to find their way across the Sahara, in search of Timbuctoo or simply of a new route not previously mapped. The desert took a terrible toll. Of some 200 travellers who ventured into it during Queen Victoria's reign, 165 died of fever, or were murdered by the Tuareg who did not welcome curious intruders.

Not unnaturally they also failed to admit that a force stronger than themselves had eventually appeared along the fringes of their territory. The French, during the last century, were making themselves masters of Algeria; for half a century they kept to the cultivated and mountain lands of the northern coastal region, but, little by little, they began to move southwards. In 1880 a small mission led by Colonel Flatters was sent southwards to survey the line for a projected railway from Paris to Timbuctoo. In the central Sahara they were surrounded by Tuareg, but managed to slip away. Continuing their work, the following year, they were less fortunate and eighty-five men perished at the hands of the Tuareg.

The French were not accustomed to tolerate that kind of opposition to their 'mission civilisatrice' and began to organise companies of specialised desert troops, mounted on camels as were the Tuareg, but better trained and better armed. They were recruited from nomad herdsmen and led by French officers. They burst on the Sahara with a victory whose fame echoed through the desert. In 1902, a company of 140 of these desert troops, led by one Frenchman, met a far larger force of Tuareg at Tit in the Hoggar. At the end of the day, 150 Tuareg lay dead on the battlefield, while the French-led forces had lost only four men.

The Tuareg learnt from this event that they should treat the newcomers with caution and respect. As the small French companies extended the range of their operations throughout what is now the Algerian Sahara, the Tuareg, by and large, left them in peace. When there were reverses, the French were quick to avenge them, so that by the outbreak of World War I the French companies had explored most of the desert and had acquired a fund of experience in desert warfare.

With the outbreak of World War I, the desert flared into renewed fighting, the nomads led now by the Sanusi of Cyrenaica in Libya. But they were not able to oust the tenacious foreigners from their midst, and after the war the French companies settled down again to their patient desert patrols, aimed at eliminating slave trading and raiding from the lands of the desert tribes. Eventually they used motorised columns increasingly more often, but for much of the difficult desert terrain the camel was still the only practical means of access.

To the east, in Libya, a more bitter, life-and-death struggle was played out during these years, between the Sanusi with their bedouin followers and other European invaders, the Italians. The Italians had first tried to establish their rule in Libya in 1911 without great success; from 1923 to 1932 they waged a war with no holds barred against the bedouin whom they must conquer if they were to establish farms for Italian settlers, to relieve poverty back home. When the Fascist government came to power in Italy, it was determined to succeed at any cost.

It was this war, more than any other struggle, which demonstrated the bedouin vulnerability to modern methods of warfare. In the open desert, where, before World War I, the bedouin had virtually always had the upper hand and had been practically invulnerable, since only other bedouin troops (such as those used in the French desert companies) could reach them, there was now no protection against planes armed with bombs and machine-guns. The black tents, lying low in hollows out of sight of a camel rider, were highly conspicuous from the air. Whole camps – men, women, children and their flocks and herds – could be eliminated within a few minutes, and no amount of courage could save them. Surprise raids across the desert by mechanised units could achieve the same effect and armed columns would fall on a camp and massacre everyone in it.

The bedouin losses in the open desert plains were appalling, as is shown even in the Italian statistics which are considered open to question. In six months of 1923, the Italians estimated that 800 bedouin were killed, 1,000 wounded, and 700 camels and 22,000 sheep killed or confiscated. By 1927 the Italians put the bedouin losses for the year at 1,296 killed, 2,844 camels and 5,000 sheep slaughtered, and some 19,000 animals confiscated.

Very many more bedouin died in the concentration camps into which they were herded during the later years of the war. By 1930 some 80,000 bedouin and 600,000 animals were living in these camps where disease and malnutrition took a very heavy toll. The bedouin, used to the freedom of the open desert, could not live in this abject confinement. Many died simply of a broken heart; their animals died for lack of food.

Nevertheless, throughout this time the bedouin bands managed to keep up a continual guerrilla warfare against the Italians, under the leadership of the aged but indomitable Sidi Umar al Mukhtar. He saw that in the open desert, however remote, his men had no chance against the Italian planes and mechanised columns. He therefore concentrated his

40 Gathering of the tribes in Kuwait during Colonel Dickson's days when the motor car had come to supplement the horse and camel in desert travel and warfare (*Middle East Centre, Oxford*)

efforts on the rugged wooded plateau where gorges, caves and abrupt mountains offered good natural cover. From hideouts in this region his men continued to harrass the Italians.

The end came in 1931 when Sidi Umar was wounded, captured and later hanged. The defeated bedouin tried to flee across the desert into Egypt, but their caravans were bombed and machine-gunned from the air, and only remnants of their people escaped. It was clear that, in the modern world of advanced technology, traditional bedouin military strength could be no match for the armies, and especially the airforce, of a strong central government.

Nowhere else was bedouin power brought to so traumatic an end, nor so deliberately destroyed, as in Libya. Elsewhere the process was a gradual adaptation by the bedouin to increasing restrictions on their liberty and autonomy, a gradual awareness that the deserts in which they alone had been masters were now open to outsiders whose ruling they must accept.

In Syria, Jordan and Iraq

Up to and during World War I, the bedouin's position remained undiminished in the deserts of Arabia and the neighbouring lands. The Turks were still the masters of much of the area, as they had been for nearly four centuries, but they had never really controlled the desert. They held many of the towns, and they protected the pilgrim route and their own supply lines with a series of forts; adequate subsidies to the shaikhs of tribes along these routes bought their acquiescence. Beyond the range of the city garrisons and the desert forts, the Turks wielded little effective control.

The British first took an interest in the Arab deserts because of their enmity to the Turks, against whom they came into open battle in World War I. A regular British army swept north out of Egypt and drove the Turkish troops before it through Palestine; another opposed the Turks in the region that is now Iraq. Best known of all, perhaps, was the desert campaign in which Lawrence of Arabia, aided by the sons of Sherif Husain of Mecca, led the bedouin tribes of the Hejaz northwards out of

Arabia, to overthrow the Turkish garrisons in what is now Jordan, and, as their crowning success, to take Damascus.

In practice the campaign may have added little to the success of Britain's war effort against the Turks. The army advancing through Palestine would certainly have taken Damascus if the bedouin forces had not done so, and the fall of the city would have cut the life-line of the Hejaz railway to the Turkish troops in Arabia. Nevertheless, it demonstrated the existing military power of the bedouin, and their ability to free their own land of the alien rulers. It also forged close links between the British, the sons of Sherif Husain, and the bedouin.

After the war the Arabs expected that they would now be masters in the lands which the Turks had vacated, but the League of Nations decided otherwise. Nation states were created from the provinces of the old Turkish empire, and Britain and France were given mandatory powers over the states until such time as they should be considered 'ready for independence'. Britain was given the mandates for Palestine, Transjordan and Iraq; France those for Syria and Lebanon.

Palestine and Lebanon were largely settled countries, but strong and powerful tribes roamed the deserts of Syria, Iraq and Transjordan (now Jordan). The British and French authorities were not particularly hostile to these tribes; indeed, the British had come to be where they were with the tribes' support. But the Europeans were accustomed to an orderly existence. They set about establishing the way of life and social systems which they knew at home, and which they were convinced were best for other people also. Inevitably, the bedouin free-wheeling lawlessness was bound to come into conflict with this disciplined central authority.

Towards the end of World War I also, the means had become available by which a strong government could at last exert real control in the desert. Lawrence had begun his campaign on camel-back; he bumped up to Damascus in a Rolls-Royce car. Amazingly, these early cars managed to keep going over rough terrain which today is better tackled in a jeep. They offered new possibilities of rapid armed attack in remote districts, and were backed by the impressive power brought to the government by aeroplanes. In the 1920s, the deserts around the northern and western fringes of Arabia were crossed and re-crossed by car; the first Citroens traversed the Sahara as far south as Timbuctoo in 1922.

The mandatory powers set about demarcating the frontiers of the new states which had been created after the war. This brought an unwelcome curb to the bedouin who were not happy to accept the significance of imaginary lines drawn across their deserts. Gradually the foreigners' patrols penetrated the northern and western deserts more and more; in their desire to provide security for their own cars and convoys, they interfered increasingly with tribal warfare and raiding. An orderly state could hardly tolerate private wars in its deserts.

By the mid-1930s, the writ of the central government ran right through the deserts of the mandatory territories. In Syria the French had established an administrative department called the *Contrôle Bédouin*. This office supervised annual migrations, settled disputes among the bedouin and between them and settled folk, and attempted to disarm the tribes when they moved into settled areas. It organised posts, patrols and mechanised units to keep the peace in the desert, and also tried to offer some social services and welfare to the nomads. Summer schools were opened in the desert for bedouin children, new wells were dug, and some clinics were set up in bedouin areas.

A severe drought in 1932 caused the death of many thousands of the bedouin's animals, and the general world depression also weakened their selling position. Thy became poorer than ever, and this also weakened the power of the tribes. J.B.Glubb, writing in 1935, said that there had been great famine and distress during the previous three or four years, and that all bedouin were 'pathetically poor' so that some, for the first time, had had to turn to hired labour to keep their families alive. About that time raids came to an end in the Jordanian desert, 'for the simple reason', Kirkbride wrote, 'that they no longer paid'.

In Iraq, in those years, the tribes were fanned to revolt from time to time by rival political parties, but the government showed that such risings, if tackled with speed and determination, could be stamped out completely. When the Beni Izrayj tribe destroyed the railway line at Rumaytha, between Baghdad and Basra, and seized government offices there, the army moved south swiftly, the tribesmen were bombed from the air, and were soon fleeing in panic.

Raiding died out completely in the deserts of Syria and Iraq in the 1940s. The tribes disliked the interference by the central government which followed such raids, and found that they could live undisturbed in their deserts only if they did not attract attention to themselves. The gap between their armaments and those of the government forces widened with the greater sophistication in weaponry which became available to the central governments during World War II. In Iraq, by 1950, an observer could write: 'The tribes were in fact, for the first time and for ever, militarily helpless.'

In Arabia

In Arabia, whence the Arab revolt against the Turks had been launched, the situation was quite different. The arid deserts of the Arabian peninsula were tribal territory *par excellence*; nomadic tribes made up the great majority of the population, and the land was so desperately poor that no mandatory powers were in the least interested in taking it under their tutelage. Ironically, the very same country (now Saudi Arabia) is today one of the richest lands in the world in per capita income, thanks to the discovery of oil.

At the time of World War I, three separate and rival states flourished in Arabia as mentioned in the last chapter. They were centred on three small towns, but their power rested in the tribes which supported them. To the north was the state of the Ibn Rashid, leaders of the Shammar tribe, with their capital at Hail. The centre and the east was the domain of their long-standing enemies the Ibn Saud, from the Anazah tribes, with their capital at Riyadh. The west was the territory of the Sherif Husain of Mecca, least tribal of the three but depending all the same on the tribes of the Hejaz for support.

At the beginning of the century the Ibn Rashid were in the ascendant. They had driven the Ibn Saud out of Riyadh and placed a governor of their own in the town's mud-brick fort. The Ibn Saud had sought refuge in Kuwait where a young son of their leading family, Abd al Aziz, grew up in exile. In 1902, at the age of twenty, he rode across the desert on camel-back with forty armed followers. They slipped into the walled town of Riyadh at night, and in the morning stormed the governor's fort. In half an hour the battle was over and Riyadh restored to the Ibn Saud dynasty.

For some twenty years the three states were to be locked in spasmodic warfare, fanned at times by the opposing powers, Britain and Turkey. The Turks were established in force in the west until the latter part of World War I, during which their position as supporters of the Sherif Husain was usurped by the British. The Ibn Rashid allied with the Turks, and to counteract this help Ibn Saud signed a treaty with Britain in 1915.

The battles fought in Arabia meanwhile were purely tribal ones. Each of the leaders sought to win the various tribes to his own side; when he took the field, it was with a smallish force of townsmen and thousands of bedouin warriors. As throughout history, the allegiance of the tribes was fickle, and their support might be won, or bought, first by one, then by another.

From the early part of his reign, Abd al Aziz Ibn Saud sought to establish something more stable than the typical bedouin power base. His family had traditionally been linked with the dynamic Wahhabi religious revival, a puritannical interpretation of Islam which had first swept the peninsula, allied to the military leadership of the Ibn Saud family, in the eighteenth century. Once firmly established in Riyadh, Abd al Aziz launched a further Wahhabi revival and aimed to carry it through the tribes, giving them a broader-based loyalty than their purely tribal one.

Special settlements for the bedouin, called *hijra*, were the cornerstone of this revival. These settlements were designed to serve several purposes at once: they would give the bedouin a more secure livelihood based on agriculture – Abd al Aziz provided them with wells and farmland; they would enable the Wahhabi faith to be preached more effectively than it could be among nomads; and they would provide a reliable, well trained reserve.

The *hijra* were organised like a military regime, with one section of the community always on instant call in case of war, a second group on stand-by, and a third group which would be called out only in case of general mobilisation. The first *hijra* was established in 1912, and Abd al Aziz was to found 122 such settlements, covering all the tribal areas, during his lifetime.

The inhabitants of the settlements were known as the *Ikhwan*, the 'Brothers' (Muslim Brotherhood in English). The combination of intense religious teaching and strong military discipline to which they were exposed forged them into fearless, fanatical fighting men who were to carry Abd al Aziz's banner throughout Arabia. He is reported to have said that originally '. . . the urban community was more determined and stronger in battle than the desert community, but now the bedouin inhabitants of the settlements are more determined and more ready for martyrdom'. They became known for their willingness to hurl themselves, with no thought for their own lives, on more numerous and better armed enemy forces.

By the end of World War I, the Turks were out of the peninsula: Abd al Aziz had expelled them from the eastern districts, and Sherif Husain's sons had thrown them out of the west. The only tenuous check on the rival states was the British support of both Ibn Saud and Sherif Husain. There was now nothing to prevent an onslaught on the territory of the Ibn Rashid and, with his superior troops, Abd al Aziz launched a campaign against them which, after nearly a year of fighting, brought Hail and the Shammar territory under this rule. Some of his *Ikhwan* troops swept onto the west and north, and almost reached Amman in Transjordan, killing the inhabitants of a village there on the way. But there they ran into forces of a quite different order, and were rapidly overwhelmed by British aeroplanes and armoured cars.

Against other bedouin troops and Arabian townsmen, however, they were invincible. In 1919 both Sherif Husain and Abd al Aziz laid claim to the same town in western Arabia. Husain sent his army of 4,000 troops; Abd al Aziz sent a far smaller force of *Ikhwan*. The latter descended on Husain's army as it camped at night and killed all but 100, who managed to make good their escape.

Five years later, the British stopped the £60,000 annual subsidy which they had been paying to Abd al Aziz, and there was no further reason for him to hold his hand against Sherif Husain. His *Ikhwan* marched west and camped before the small town of Taif; Husain's troops in the town saw the feared *Ikhwan* and withdrew, leaving the town defenceless. The *Ikhwan* entered peacefully but were fired on by mistake and, thinking they were betrayed, went on a rampage of murder and looting. As soon as their leaders reached the town they were brought under control and no further episodes of the kind were allowed to happen during the conquest of Sherif Husain's territory which followed, but it was a warning of the latent dangers of these fanatical troops.

Once all opponents within Arabia had been defeated, the *Ikhwan* were determined to carry their arms against the non-Wahhabis beyond the frontiers and the infidel British living with them. Ibn Saud forbade raids into Iraq, Kuwait and Transjordan, for he realised that air power was more than the bedouin could oppose, and feared retaliatory air raids on his own territory. But the confident *Ikhwan*, under their great leader, Faisal al Dawish, paramount shaikh of the Mutayr tribe, would brook no control. On several occasions they crossed the borders into Kuwait and Iraq, only to be driven back by the British Airforce.

Finally, in 1930, they were trapped between Abd al Aziz's forces, using cars and machine-guns, lying in wait for them on the Arabian side of the Kuwait frontier, and the British planes bombing their camps on the Kuwaiti side into which they had crossed. With bombs falling all round on his tents, Faisal al Dawish was finally obliged to surrender to the British, and was sent, a prisoner, to Riyadh were he died two years later. The military corps of the *Ikhwan* was dissolved, and many abandoned the settlements and returned, embittered, to their tribes.

It was now time for Abd al Aziz, who was declared king of the new state of Saudi Arabia, to bring all the tribes of the peninsula under his control, and to establish his authority throughout his territory. He banned attacks on caravans, raiding and the extortion of *khuwa* (protection money); and built up his own strength with cars (whose import into the kingdom was restricted) and aeroplanes (which could not be owned by private persons until well after World War II).

He knew that, to control the tribes of Arabia, who throughout the centuries had been the least subject to restraint, he must show that he meant what he said, and that he was capable of enforcing it. When the

Beni Harb tribe of the Hejaz defied his ban and carried out a fierce raid, taking a large amount of plunder, he despatched his troops with great speed to attack the Harb camp without mercy. Some 200 Harb tribesmen were killed, and the news of the swift and severe punishment rang through the deserts. A few similar actions on a smaller scale sufficed to bring the tribes to heel and, having recognised a master whom they could not disobey, they were to become his most loyal followers.

King Abd al Aziz was perhaps the last of the great tribal leaders of the old school. He controlled the bedouin by a mixture of strength and diplomacy, winning the tribes by his force of leadership and by military power, and holding them by generosity and by marrying the daughters of tribal shaikhs to establish a blood relationship. In him the bedouin found a leader they could admire and had to respect.

Well before his death in old age, observers wrote that the contrast between the Arabia of the past and of the latter part of his reign was 'incredible'. Raiding and tolls were forgotten; travellers could move about unmolested; the whole huge kingdom of thinly populated deserts was subject to the rule of law and obedient to his word. It is also true that, through this great leader whom they learned to obey, the bedouin finally lost their freedom of action and autonomy in the modern state of Saudi Arabia.

9

THE BEDOUIN IN THE MODERN STATE

Ask a townsman in the Middle East about the bedouin and, as likely as not, the answer will be that there are no more bedouin. The bedouin impact on the towns has faded fast in the past few decades. Townsmen are no longer in fear of their attacks, they travel in the desert without let or hindrance, they can buy their meat frozen or imported on the hoof from abroad, and they are no longer aware of the nomads coming into their markets.

In part this is because the nomads themselves are no longer particularly distinguishable from the settled people. A bedouin driving a pick-up truck into town, dressed in clothes which he has bought in the markets of the town, looks scarcely different from a townsman – even if his load is half a dozen sheep or a few goats. Anywhere near the fringes of the desert, or the asphalt roads, it is far more common to see bedouin driving lorries or pick-ups than to see them riding camels.

It is also true that the bedouin are gradually disappearing from the deserts. Each year there are fewer of them; each year they accept further changes in their way of life. Yet they could not disappear from the Arab deserts without trace, as though they had never been, in the way that gipsies, for instance, might do from the British countryside. For the bedouin are not an alien impoverished society, living on the fringe of a stronger sedentary culture in the Middle East; on the contrary, they are the basis of Arabian culture and society; their values are still often the ones which are accepted and admired in the cities today; their language is considered the best Arabic, their poetry the best literature. If they were to vanish from the deserts, it would leave the Arab lands like a garden from which the oldest tree had been uprooted. Young trees would continue to sprout, the direction of many of them shaped by their former relationship to the old tree, but something fundamental would have gone and it would be a very long time before the gap would heal over.

The bedouin today are not very numerous. Perhaps they never were very numerous, since the deserts could never have supported a really large nomadic population, and their influence and power was certainly out of proportion to their numbers. No one has ever managed to count the nomads successfully; not only are they always on the move, but also they are highly suspicious of government officials who come to ask questions. If they thought that the questions might lead to military service or taxation, they might give a lower answer; if they felt it might lead to subsidies or social welfare, they might give a higher answer. They would probably not think of mentioning their women and girls, and no official could go into the women's part of the tents to count heads.

A few years ago, an official, who was sent to count the wild Chehu tribe in the northern mountains of the United Arab Emirates, was met by a blank refusal to co-operate. 'If you set foot in our mountains, we shall shoot you', they warned, for they suspected military service was the goal. Prudently he retired, but, soon after, the Chehu heard that subsidies were being issued to tribes in the south. Perhaps that was the cause of the census? They sent to find the official who by now was counting a more amenable tribe. 'Come and count us', they ordered. He demurred, only to receive the warning: 'If you don't come and count us we shall shoot you.'

So estimates only are available for the number of bedouin in the deserts today, just as mere estimates are available for those in the last century. Nevertheless, most estimates agree that the numbers today are low: one specialist remarks that they come to not much more than 1 per cent of the total population of the Arab Middle East (of about 120 million), and this may well be fairly near the truth. In the 1960s there were estimated to be about a quarter of a million bedouin in Iraq, slightly more in Syria, and about 100,000 in Jordan. In Egypt and the Sahara the numbers now are relatively low, estimated in the 1960s at a quarter of a million in the Maghreb, a little less than that in Libya, and under 70,000 in the Western Desert of Egypt. Briggs put the number of Tuareg at a mere 10–20,000. The only state where there were thought to be large numbers of bedouin is Saudi Arabia.

In the past, estimates of the Saudi population gave half to two-thirds of the people as nomadic; recent estimates put the number of bedouin at around 600,000 out of an indigenous population of perhaps 4 million. In all these countries, the numbers are dropping fast as the bedouin find more lucrative work in the towns, or settle down to cultivate the land.

Nevertheless, they have a useful role to play as nomadic herders in the economies of the modern states. They alone can make use of vast areas of land (in some Arab states up to 90 per cent of the land is desert) which no one else is willing or able to exploit. They can produce a much needed supply of meat, milk and cheese from land which is otherwise unusable, thanks to their age-old knowledge of the desert. In the eastern Arab countries of Iraq, Syria, Jordan and Saudi Arabia, there are some 14 million sheep, 4 million goats and 650,000 camels (FAO estimates), largely kept by the bedouin, although many goats are also kept by townspeople.

The demand for meat has risen rapidly in all the Middle Eastern countries, with the increasing prosperity brought by the discovery of oil. Lands like Saudi Arabia, once net exporters of animals, now themselves import large numbers (well over a million a year) from the south, the Sudan and Somalia, and the demand is continually rising with the increasing numbers of immigrants and pilgrims who come to the country. In recent years the major demand has been for sheep, and (as the above figures show) the bedouin have adapted to this. Lately the demand for camels has also risen, but the bedouin herds are insufficient to meet it.

There is no doubt that the bedouin can today find a ready market for every animal they can rear. There are, however, various constraints on their ability to produce, which might be overcome – in part at least –

although perhaps only with outside help. Most serious of these is over-grazing of the desert range. Plant life in the desert depends precariously on occasional showers of rain; these may occur in any given area only at intervals of a year, or even of several years. If grazing is controlled so that plants are not eaten right down to the root, then they will recover with time. But if animals are allowed to graze too long in any one place, the plants will not recover, and the grazing ground will revert to completely barren desert.

In recent years, a number of factors have combined to tempt the bedouin to overgraze their land. Today instant relief from lack of water or grazing is offered by the pick-up truck. The camp can stay where it is, while the man of the family goes off to collect all the water needed in old oil-drums. Or he loads his flocks into the back of the truck and drives them off a few miles across the desert to a better area, returning to the camp with them at night. Gradually he collects more and more belongings in his camp, and so is loath to move more often than is absolutely essential.

The new government wells in the desert have also added to this problem. These wells were dug to relieve the pressure of demand on the water supply which was one of the most frequent causes of fighting in the desert. They are open to all bedouin, and none can prevent another from using them. They have been dug in areas where there was water below ground, and often where there is good grazing. The bedouin can camp some distance from the wells and fetch water each day for their flocks, again without moving their camp. As a result the grazing has been eaten to the ground in an increasingly wide circle around the wells.

Various government measures have also discouraged the bedouin from caring for the desert rangelands in the past half century. The frontiers between states, drawing new lines across the deserts, marked one step in that direction. Although the bedouin crossed them to graze, they felt that the land on the other side of the frontier was alien, not theirs, and therefore might as well be grazed right down. In Saudi Arabia the government abolished, in 1953, the tribal grazing rights to a given area, preserved until then by the *hema* system. This made grazing available to all, but meant that no one group felt responsible for its management any longer. Why deprive one's own flocks to preserve the plants, when next week someone else might come and graze them down to the ground?

Another field in which bedouin stock-herding could be improved is that of marketing. Traditionally the bedouin have always come into the towns once a year to sell their year's surplus of animals. Today they continue to do the same. Hamad of the Harb goes into the city once a year and sells his young camels for between £1–200 a time; the quoted selling price for adult camels in the market seems to be £4–500. In many cases the bedouin could obtain a better price for their animals if they were to keep them longer and sell them at a different time of the year.

In fact, today the bedouin rely far more on outside sources for their cash incomes than on their animals. In a recent study of the Liwa oasis in Abu Dhabi, Franke Heard-Bey found that almost every one of the bedouin men there had taken paid employment at some time or another. And every bedouin family which visited the oasis had at least one son working for the government. Very often another son worked in the defence forces or in business, while a third might run a taxi in the town. Meanwhile the father of the family continued to lead the traditional life and to care for the family's animals. The sons still kept close links with their families, and came to visit the oasis when they could.

The bedouin standard of living and general comfort has certainly risen in recent years. They enjoy complete peace and security, and are no longer in fear of the catastrophic loss of their whole herd in a sudden raid. It is now worth their while to build up good, well bred herds. The income from outside enables them to enjoy luxuries from outside also, such as tinned foods which are well adapted to keeping in the desert, and which provide more flavour and variety to bedouin meals than was ever enjoyed before. Tinned milk powder is also much appreciated and ensures against their children starving when the flocks fail to produce sufficient milk.

Trucks, radios, paraffin lamps and cookers all make life easier and more pleasant, and give the bedouin a wider range of experience and interest. At the time of the discoveries of the ancient scrolls in the caves beside the Dead Sea, for instance, the bedouin who found them were able to keep themselves informed of the market prices of these rare items, thanks to their radios. Binoculars and the compass ease the traditional tasks of herding and making one's way around the desert. I recently explained, somewhat patronisingly, the workings of a compass to some bedouin boys who had asked me what I was holding. They took the instrument and looked at it critically. 'Your compass is quite accurate,' one said earnestly to me, 'since the needle points north to the *jebel* (mountain) over there.' All their people now used compasses (this was about a hundred miles from Al Medina) when travelling by truck, they claimed.

Despite these additional comforts, which are much appreciated by the nomads, the gap between their standard of living and that of the settled people is widening rapidly. Oil has brought wealth to the countries of the Middle East, and this has largely been concentrated in the towns. When money does come to the nomads, they do not save or invest it; they may give a feast to their relatives, or offer the bride-money for their son to marry, or buy new clothes. Soon they are without funds again, and borrowing in the towns at extortionate rates of interest.

A serious handicap, which helps to widen the gap between the nomad and the townsman, is the high illiteracy rate of the bedouin. Schooling is difficult to provide for nomadic desert dwellers and, despite the fact that most governments have made considerable efforts in this direction, a large number of nomad children still grow up unable to read or write. This leaves them at a disadvantage with the townsman in any kind of business dealing, and also restricts them in their choice of work when they do go to the towns.

Ambitious boys who leave the tribes must seek education as one of their first steps towards a sedentary life. Salih, for instance, is the son of a semi-nomadic shepherd family in southern Arabia. He and his ten brothers and sisters had no schooling at home in their tent, but when any of them moved to the towns they quickly enrolled in night school. Two boys and two girls stayed with their father and their flocks; the rest learnt to read and write and all the boys took jobs in offices in the big cities. Salih prefers the country district where his father lives to the city, but would not like to be a shepherd himself.

Young men like Salih face other problems than those of acquiring

133

education and employment. The strict social code by which they were brought up is difficult to apply to life in the cities. Traditionally, a bedouin's status depended on his bravery in raids and battle, his generosity and ability to extend hospitality, and the honour of the women of his family. Military prowess can now be exhibited only through service in the armed forces, and has vanished from the daily life of the tribes. Hospitality is still the route to status in the desert, but it is far more difficult for a young ex-bedouin clerk or taxi driver to offer a whole sheep to his guests (at a cost of £60–70) than it is for a young shepherd who can kill one of his own lambs. All bedouin men have had to adapt to a new concept of their role in life; for those who have settled in the towns, the adaptation is far greater and more disturbing.

Another weakness in the bedouin's position today is their relative lack of participation in national life. By and large they live a life apart, diverging more and more from the increasingly complex life of the cities. Traditionally they have always had direct access to the *majlis* of the ruler of the state, and in the past have made use of this to come to express their troubles and grievances. But, as state business increases, and heads of state and their officials find their time ever more heavily occupied, they become less willing and able to give access to any bedouin who seeks to see them. This direct personal contact with their leader is the only social system which the bedouin know and understand; they are daunted by the difficulties of working through the bureaucracy.

It requires great efforts on the part of the central government to include the bedouin in the life of the state. Social services can be brought to them only at disproportionate cost, both in money and in effort; a census is a really major undertaking; taxes can be collected only with great difficulty; their opinion sought only by mounting a massive expedition. In 1976, for instance, when the Algerian government wished to collect the votes of the bedouin in a referendum on the National Charter, lorries with mobile polling stations had to be despatched into the Sahara to seek out the few and widespread tent dwellers and started polling four days in advance of the rest of the country.

Only in the armed forces, it seems, are the bedouin now fully integrated into the life of the state, and here their role is often a vital one.

Service in the armed forces has provided the bedouin with a natural extension to their traditional occupation as desert warriors, and they have proved very willing and able to adapt to the technology of modern weapons. In states with a traditional regime, their loyalty to the king is unquestioned, and their support for him has at times proved decisive.

Jordan, for instance, has an army built up largely of bedouin troops. They are staunch supporters of King Husain, great-grandson of Sherif Husain of Mecca. In 1970, Jordan was wracked by civil war between the well armed Palestinian factions and the state army. Since the king could rely completely on the loyalty of his troops, he was able to risk sending them into battle within his capital of Amman, and his forces rapidly won the day. The armed Palestinians were expelled, or at least prevented from continuing military activities in Jordan.

Six years later, a comparable conflict took place in the very different state of Lebanon. There the loyalty of the army, drawn from the towns and villages, was divided; the army split and could play no effective role. The conflict dragged on for over a year, and was only quenched by the intervention of the Syrian army.

In Saudi Arabia the bedouin also play a key military role through the National Guard. There are, effectively, two armed forces in the state: the national army which is composed of townsmen and is generally stationed around border areas to protect the kingdom from outside attack, and the National Guard, composed almost entirely of bedouin troops, which is stationed throughout the land to provide internal security. The army comes under the Ministry of Defence, and the National Guard under the direct control of the king's brother.

Service in the National Guard provides the tribes with a large part of their income, and offers a very acceptable career to their young men. Their loyalty to the king is unquestioned, and they are highly trained and well armed. Through their National Guard service, men from different tribes learn to work and serve with each other, thus helping to break down traditional tribal hostilities.

Individual bedouin have also made successful careers as fighter pilots in the air forces of these states. Although a modern jet plane may seem a very far cry from the camel which their fathers used, today's young bedouin have shown themselves capable of making the colossal leap from one extreme in the field of transport to the other. A young bedouin jet pilot explained to me that he had spent his early childhood in the tent with the tribes, but in the severe drought of the late 1950s his father's herds had died. Sadly his father made his way to the city, where he sent his children to school because they were so much under his feet in the unaccustomed confined circumstances of a small house. The boys did well, one becoming an officer in the army, the other commander of a jet squadron. 'We are very lucky in our generation to have known both ways of life', the young pilot remarked.

The continuing military role of the tribes assures for them a certain power in the state which it is difficult to assess. The large, noble bedouin tribes, such as the Rwala, the Shammar and others of this kind, are certainly still a power which the central governments must take into account. Bedouin herdsmen have the right to carry arms in the desert, and such tribes can muster large numbers of trained armed men on their own account.

Their political influence is probably strongest in the states which still have a traditional regime, such as Jordan and Saudi Arabia, but they are certainly not without influence in some of the revolutionary states as well. Their influence is not exerted directly and overtly, through official representatives or departments in ministries, for example. It is managed through the old system of the pyramidal structure of the bedouin tribe, whose apex, the paramount shaikh, now has his residence in the city; his brothers, sons and nephews meanwhile, may still be living with the tribe, whom he will also visit frequently.

The shaikh makes it his business to keep in close contact with members of the ruling family or the ruling hierarchy. In matters which affect the interest of the tribe, his representations will receive serious consideration, especially when the tribe is a large and powerful one. The paramount shaikh of the Rwala, for example, lives in Damascus and has a house in Amman. Although Syria is ruled by a revolutionary, military government, the views of a cohesive, well armed tribe such as the Rwala cannot be disregarded. The weight which is given to them can be increased by the negotiating skill of the shaikh.

Tribal influence can be exerted in another way. The support of a large tribe can increase the power of an individual prince or member of a government. He may offer them subsidies from his own pocket to encourage their support; in return for their allegiance he will try to foster their interests in the central government. The opportunities offered to different tribes in military service, for instance, can depend on the word of a well placed prince.

Open conflict has not arisen between the tribes and the various central governments for many years now. This may be due both to the tribes' awareness that eventual victory must go to the government, as well as to the governments' desire to live in peace with the tribes. The governments give generous subsidies to the tribes, both as a way of distributing the national wealth to a section of the population who would otherwise have little share in it, and in order to keep their allegiance. While some subsidies, such as those on livestock, are fixed, most are spasmodic. In cases of drought or emergency the government gives a large sum to the tribes or individuals concerned. But the gift may not be repeated another year; the bedouin cannot rely on receiving this bounty and when they have done, erroneously, it has led them into worse troubles.

Individual bedouin can usually obtain a gift or a loan to meet their needs or to purchase some expensive equipment such as a truck or a water tanker. They can appeal to their shaikh, to the governor of their district, or to a prince, and will often receive a favourable hearing. But these subsidies, like the government ones, cannot be relied on. If the bedouin is lucky he comes away with a brand-new truck; if he is a little less lucky he has the truck but must pay back the capital and sometimes a considerable interest as well; if he is unlucky he gets nothing. Depending on government and individual gifts is as unpredictable for him as depending on the rainfall is for his flocks.

The general attitude of the governments to the tribes is rather ambivalent. The tribes can be useful and a source of strength, they must be kept quiet and happy and this is most readily done by handouts, but life would be easier and more orderly if only they would just melt away. Such hand-outs to the tribes are not a new feature of government in desert lands: the Romans paid the tribes along their frontiers to ensure the security of their empire; the Turks paid the tribes along the major caravan routes, especially the pilgrim routes.

There are social disadvantages to this method of distributing wealth. It can be seen as a form of charity which diminishes the individual bedouin's self-respect on the one hand, and which fails to encourage him to greater productivity on the other. For many years, therefore, governments have felt that perhaps a better way of tackling the poverty of the bedouin was to encourage them to settle: to cease, in fact, to be bedouin at all.

10

SETTLEMENT OF THE BEDOUIN

All round the tractor's rumbling
Reassures more than the camel's grumbling.
On the primus the tea pot is boiling,
In the cupboard the glasses shine without spoiling.

Song of a settled bedouin girl
(adapted from a government paper on settlement of nomads)

King Husain of Jordan, in his autobiography, *Uneasy Lies the Head*, described a visit which he made to a bedouin camp early in his reign. He
was shocked by the poverty and hardship of the bedouin's life, and determined to do all he could to help them escape the harshness of their
existence. Many other rulers and administrators throughout the Middle
East have felt as King Husain did when they considered the thin, undernourished, ill clad bodies of the nomads, and saw how pathetically subject they were to unnecessary sudden death in times of drought, in
infancy, in childbirth, and from appendicitis, snake bite and accident.

For several decades, therefore, it has been the policy of Middle Eastern
governments to encourage the settlement of the bedouin. As nomadic
stock-herders, their standard of living remains distressingly low, their
average annual income being always below that of settled people. Recently they have become more and more dependent on government
subsidies or payments of one sort or another to make ends meet. Their

physical condition was probably not much better in the past than it is now—and may, indeed, have been worse; but the difference between their standard of living and that of the sedentary population was not great. Oasis cultivators, townsmen and villagers in most Arab countries were also desperately poor: their life had little extra to offer that would attract a nomad.

Today, however, the discovery of oil has brought sudden amazing wealth to many Arab countries. The greatest wealth has come to those states which were previously the poorest and often had the largest bedouin populations: Arabia, Libya, Iraq and the tiny Gulf States. The wealth has gone to the settled population and, since World War II, the gap between the lives of the nomads and those of the city dwellers has intensified sharply; in the last ten years it has widened to a great gulf. Today, townspeople are educated, part of a complex society, aware of the world and national and international affairs; the nomad, while his horizons have certainly widened, is still generally illiterate, his personal experience limited to the care of his animals and existence in the empty desert.

Governments have seen that more and more welfare and assistance would be needed by their nomadic populations, and have judged that the nomads'contribution to the economic life of the state would not merit this. Yet a dissatisfied, elusive and mobile population, within the boundaries and yet not part of their state, is not a prospect which most governments can regard with equanimity. The nomads, if they become disaffected, could provide a basis for infiltration from outside, not to mention a disturbing element in their own right. They must be integrated and kept reasonably content.

The obvious way to achieve these ends, it was thought, was to provide them with land, encourage them to cultivate it, and so chain them to the soil. King Abd al Aziz Ibn Saud of Arabia was the first to launch this policy on a wide scale with his *Ikhwan* settlements, and these were also perhaps the first to illustrate the difficulties facing such a policy. Agriculture in the desert is a hard and unrewarding task; if it is to pay, it needs special skills and must often be carried out professionally and on a large scale. It is no job for luke-warm amateurs.

The nomads throughout the ages have despised cultivators and regarded any form of hard physical labour, especially on the land, as a menial task degrading to noble bedouin. For them to agree to try to cultivate the land at all, a radical shift of opinion was needed. For them to undertake the reclamation of new land, which in most cases was what it amounted to, far more than a change of heart was involved. The reclamation of former desert requires back-breaking work and for several years shows little reward for effort. Water must be obtained and brought to the crops, irrigation systems constructed, wind-break trees grown, the land fertilised and the plants given time to mature. It was hard for a bedouin to wait so long for a reward to his labours. It was even harder when the scheme was hit by a drop in the water table, or a drying-up of the water resources, just as it was getting established. Many of the early *Ikhwan* settlements suffered in this way: when their water reserves were exhausted, their cultivation – only partially successful in the first place – had to be abandoned.

Claude Jarvis, a particularly perceptive British administrator who worked in the Egyptian Desert in the 1930s, spelled out the problems of settling the bedouin on the land long before most of the settlement schemes were launched. He advised that the bedouin must be slowly weaned to agriculture, but warned that it was 'a most difficult and heartbreaking task'. The best approach, he found, was the development of small cheap gardens for individual bedouin. 'Big schemes, involving big masonry dams, high powered pumping plant, etc., would savour so much of government interference, intensive cultivation, an eight hour day, and all the other trammels of civilisation loathed by the Bedouin, that he would in all probability trek off into the harshest part of the desert to avoid it.' And the government, having spent so much on land reclamation, would have to settle someone else there to make it worth while.

Jarvis's forecasts have proved surprisingly accurate. Large-scale land reclamation projects, such as the Wadi Natrun in Egypt, proved prohibitively expensive and needed experienced cultivators if they were to have any chance of success. The Haradh project in Saudi Arabia, designed as a settlement scheme for bedouin, was also extremely expensive and did not attract bedouin. It is now being used as a large-scale sheep-fattening project, with little bedouin participation except as hired labour.

Smaller schemes, with a more homely atmosphere, and especially those in which plots of land were distributed to individual bedouin families, have been somewhat more successful, but the bedouin have always had a tendency to move off into the desert again with their animals, leaving their plots, if they must, to the care of old men and children.

Recently, it seems, governments are beginning to reconsider the accepted idea that the only way to solve the bedouin's problems is to settle him on the land. It is being suggested that their ability to make use of otherwise unusable land, and to produce meat and dairy products from it, should be encouraged; that perhaps help with grazing and marketing and water resources might be more productive than the simple distribution of land. Their meat production is immensely in demand today, with the rising standard of living in the cities, and their water consumption in the desert is very much lower than it would be if they were settled as cultivators. In lands where water is scarce, this is also a relevant consideration.

While government settlement schemes have not always produced the desired results, the bedouin's own taste for the comforts of settled life has brought about a massive exodus from the deserts during the past few decades. In all Middle Eastern countries a rapid drop in the numbers of bedouin has been recorded, although precise figures are not generally available. Sample surveys in Saudi Arabia, the land with the highest bedouin population, have indicated a net annual loss of 2 per cent from the nomad population of the desert.

Many of the nomads have, in fact, settled themselves on the land. Generally they reach this stage through a gradual process of specialising in sheep-rearing, abandoning their camels, moving less often and less far, and finding it worthwhile to engage in a little cultivation for part of the year. Their longing for freedom and the ability to move off at will is not hampered in the early stages of this process: at any moment they could take up their old life again.

They are attracted by the presence of new wells in the desert, and begin to camp for longer and longer periods near them. The wells along the oil pipelines running through Arabia, Iraq and Jordan have become the nuclei of small townships with unpromising names such as H4. New bedouin settlements develop in a quite different manner from traditional villages. They are immediately recognisable, for they look for all the world like a bedouin camp executed in mud brick or breeze block: each house stands alone, separated by a stretch of sand from its neighbours; clusters of houses are separated by wider stretches of sand, marking the divisions between the different family groups.

Older villages in the area, those of the original peasant farmers cluster close for protection, and even sometimes present an almost continuous external wall to the world outside. These older villages developed as groups of houses and gradually acquired a mosque, shops, a police post and a school. The bedouin settlements grow in reverse: often a well, a police post, a mosque and a school come first; the houses are added around them later.

The bedouin settlements are highly dependent on motor transport today, and bedouin cultivators take eagerly to such mechanical aids as the tractor. They have no old traditions of cultivation to overcome, and the tractor frees them from degrading physical labour. They seem to have a knack with vehicles, as they did in the past with camels, and they are all keenly interested in what goes on under the bonnets of their trucks. Their children take to driving young also, in the traffic-free environment of the desert, just as western farmers' children do in their own fields.

The decisive factor in the sedentarisation of the bedouin was the establishment of the oil companies' activities in the remotest deserts. When the companies looked around for labour to man their rigs and wells, the only source available was the bedouin. They found that bedouin were ready to learn and prepared to work hard for a regular wage. To begin with, the bedouin may have proved somewhat unreliable, moving back into the deserts as the needs of their animals dictated, but gradually individual members of the tribes opted for regular paid labour, and stayed with the companies. They sent back part of their

41 The old and new side by side: a tractor parked by a bedouin tent (*Dickins*)

wages to their families, and gradually the tents filled with modern appliances and additional belongings. The family then found it too much trouble to move frequently; they tended to remain in one spot for months on end until their flocks began to die. Eventually the flocks would be sold and the families would settle near the oil camps.

For many bedouin, oil-company money was their first taste of wage labour, but it was not to be their last. From the oil camps many moved on to the cities, or their younger brothers and cousins moved there ahead of them. Their choice of work was restricted by their lack of education, and the dislike of manual labour which made construction work unattractive, but driving offered wide opportunities. Many bedouin have become taxi and truck drivers (in Saudi Arabia they have almost a monopoly of the taxi business), and they are also often drawn into the police and armed forces. Today many young bedouin who have gone to the cities have taken courses at night-school and work in offices, especially as government officials.

Schooling is, in fact, one of the main magnets which draws bedouin from the deserts. They are eager that their children should benefit from the free education which all states now provide, and the only way for many of them to achieve this is for the whole family to settle within a few miles of a school. Some families send their sons to stay with relatives living near a school, but, by and large, they prefer to stay with their children.

Over the ages, bedouin have always settled along the fringes of the deserts, often compelled to make the move by extreme poverty and the loss of their herds. Poverty, as well as wealth, has also driven bedouin to settle during the past few decades, especially during the extreme droughts of the late 1950s and early 1960s in Arabia, and of the early 1970s in the Sahara. In the 1940s, Montagne recounted that many newly settled bedouin were desperately poor, and that their undernourished children died in large numbers; the transition from one way of life to another was marked by a tragic wastage of human life.

Settlement is bringing another personal tragedy to many tents in the desert. It is the young men who go off to the cities to seek their fortunes, and after a while they send for their wives and young children to join them. If they are unmarried, they try to bring their sisters to the towns to keep house for them, and the old people are left in the desert alone. A stranger driving past a dismantled camp was asked by an old bedouin to help him load the tent into his pick-up because it was too heavy for him. Why, asked the stranger, had the rest of the camp not helped? They had gone ahead with the flocks, the old man replied, and indeed the stranger came across the little group some distance away. All were aged; there were no young people to help them any more.

They are luckier when the family as a whole settles gradually. I visited some tents near a market town and found only an old man, women and small children looking after the flocks of sheep and goats. The flocks were too small to support the family, and they said they relied now on

42 Two examples of the *bait as sanadiq*, house of tin boxes, which is often the nomads' first settled home. These huts stand beside more permanent dwellings to which, in time, their owners move on (*author*)

tinned milk powder. Their menfolk would be back at night; they went to work each day as motor mechanics in the town. But they were keeping their options open. If the new life did not turn out well, they could buy a few more sheep and move back to the desert at a day's notice.

The next stage of settlement is to build a little shack outside a town or village. This may be made of wood from old packing crates, of corrugated metal, or, frequently of empty tins (like large biscuit tins). The tins provide a natural layer of insulation and the huts are often given a decorative exterior by the use of layers of different-coloured tins. They are considered quite superior: an old camel-herder told me firmly that he certainly did not live in a *Bait ash Shaar* (house of hair – ie tent); he lived in a good *Bait as Sanadiq* (house of boxes – ie shack). Many recent shack dwellers keep their black tent rolled up in the corner so that they can be off at will; many more have the black tent erected beside their shack and enclose the whole with a wall of brushwood or mud brick.

When more permanent houses of mud brick are built, the same system is still often followed. The black tent stands in the little yard, ready for the shepherds to move away with the flocks or as accommodation for some (often older) members of the family for the rest of the year. Shacks, shanties and village houses are built in the first instance in family groups,

146

keeping together the social unit of the desert. But as time goes on, and one member of the family prospers more than the others with his taxi or small shop, he moves away a little and builds a better home. Class distinctions, which were unknown in the desert, begin to drive a wedge through the bedouin groups; class consciousness is born where it never existed before.

As the tribe begins to settle, the role of the shaikh alters radically too. In the past he was their counsellor, guide and leader in everyday life, in peace and in war. Today the shaikh is often the first to build himself a house in the city; he no longer lives with the tribe, and he often grows far richer than the ordinary tribesman. In some cases, tribal land somehow becomes his personal estate. He is no longer the everyday leader of the tribe, but his role as intermediary between the tribesmen and government officials develops as an important one. Sometimes the shaikh himself becomes a government official, his appointment subject to government ratification.

The process of settlement can be a traumatic one for the bedouin. Traditional society, as they have always known it, dissolves round them; the traditional figures of authority move away from them, and their absolute right of access to the leading members of their society is closed, as shaikhs, ministers and kings find life too busy to allow time to spend listening to the petty troubles of every bedouin who comes in from the desert.

Their confident feeling of equality with all men (in the tribes, after all, the shaikh was only *primus inter pares*, and wealth depended on the luck of the raid) collapses in an increasingly stratified class society. And the moral standards by which they have always lived — bravery, self-sufficiency, generosity, honour — can often no longer be maintained in the towns. Their physical hygiene suffers too: in the desert it was ensured to some extent by frequent changes of camping ground, but a shanty town easily becomes an urban slum when it is devoid of services and inhabited by people whose only knowledge of hygiene was to keep on the move.

Those concerned with the welfare of the bedouin have therefore long debated the most painless ways of effecting the transition from nomadic

43 New housing for bedouin near Hàifa (*Dickins*)

desert dweller to sedentary citizen, whether townsman or cultivator. Some have felt that the move should be swift and final, avoiding the potentially painful and unhealthy shanty-town phase and the economic problems which may accompany it. Others have felt that the transition should be a slow and gradual process of acclimatisation: a move from camel-herding to sheep-rearing to semi-nomadism to semi-settled life, leading eventually to complete acceptance of village existence.

The latter method certainly has the advantage of keeping family groups together, and even of preserving the social community of whole sections of tribes. But perhaps the opportunities for gradual settlement around the edges of the deserts cannot accommodate enough of the bedouin, perhaps success by that route comes too slowly. Today, at any rate, many bedouin are of their own choice making the sudden break, moving directly into city life with no intermediary stage.

Another open question is whether there will be any bedouin at all in the desert in the future. Many writers have forecast that in a generation's time they will be no more. The young people are leaving now; gradually the older ones who remain will die, leaving no one to replace them. Others, on the contrary, and especially those who have lived with the great bedouin tribes in recent years, have found that many of the nomads of those tribes are determined to preserve their own way of life; they can conceive of no other life which could compare with the freedom of the desert, and they have no wish to settle in the congested cities. The remaining period of great oil wealth will be the testing time, for during that period the temptation to move to the town to make their fortune will be at its greatest for the young bedouin. Much will depend, also, on whether governments genuinely decide that the bedouin contribution to the nation's meat and milk requirements is sufficiently important to preserve, and on whether they can find ways of making stock-herding an economically viable and attractive proposition. In the past, the bedouin were certainly underemployed and, indeed, a substantial proportion of their active young men spent much of their time in the non-productive pursuits of raiding and warfare. Today, a smaller number of bedouin can still maintain the same sized herds as their predecessors did. It may be that even fewer bedouin in the future will still be able to keep up, or even increase, the size of the herds: that they will accept a more active existence in order to preserve their own way of life.

Today it looks as though the great tribes have the best chances of survival. It is less attractive for a Rwala or a Shammar tribesman to become a taxi driver than it is for a member of a lesser shepherd tribe. The heroic, warlike side of their life has, presumably been lost for ever. They are no longer masters of their own deserts, able to defy all outside power, and to retreat to the inviolable inner desert in times of danger. Today the deserts have been penetrated to their innermost core, and are regularly crossed and re-crossed by trucks, jeeps and aeroplanes.

It is easy to regret the passing of the romantic figure of the noble, honourable and brave bedouin warrior, as he appears in the writings of such authors as Lawrence of Arabia and Carl Raswan. Does the reality actually justify this regret? Other travellers who have known the bedouin well have pointed out much less attractive characteristics. Doughty described them at various times as 'treacherous', 'murderous' and 'thieving'. He tells how one of them warned him: 'Beware, though, the Beduw are all robbers' and related their proverb that 'The stranger is for the wolf'. 'The bedouin are fiends' the oasis dwellers said to him.

James Wellard, writing of the Sahara in the past, remarked that the Tuareg were basically thugs and bandits, responsible for the wanton murder of many foreign travellers who penetrated the desert in the last century. Even Claude Jarvis, who made such efforts on the bedouin's behalf in the 1930s, wrote that, to those who did not know him, the bedouin seemed a 'wonderful figure of romance', while to those who did he was a 'hopeless and useless creature'.

Society today would hardly tolerate the extremes of bedouin behaviour of the past: the blood feuds, the thirst for revenge, the lack of respect for each other's property, and the extortionate demands upon those unable to defend themselves. But these are relegated now to the past, and the bedouin of today, although only two generations removed from the 'heroic age', has quite different interests and concerns. He is eager to adapt to modern life, willing to modify his own ways to take advantage of present opportunities, or even to transform his existence completely. Young people of bedouin descent are succeeding in a wide variety of careers today; their brothers and cousins who have stayed in the desert should also be able to succeed as nomadic stock-herders, if given the right encouragement.

BIBLIOGRAPHY

Briggs, Lloyd Cabot. *Tribes of the Sahara* (Harvard University Press and Oxford University Press, 1960)

Bulliet, Richard W. *The Camel and the Wheel* (Harvard University Press, 1975)

Burckhardt, J.L. *Notes on the Bedouins and Wahabys* (London, 1830, reprint New York, 1967)

——*Travels in Arabia* (London, 1829)

Cole, Donald Powell. *Nomads of the Nomads: The Al Murrah Bedouin of the Empty Quarter* (Chicago, 1975)

Dickson, H.R.P. *The Arab of the Desert* (London, 1949)

Diqs, Isaak. *A Bedouin Boyhood* (London, 1967)

Doughty, Charles: *Travels in Arabia Deserta* (London, 1885)

Giraud, E. in *Sang* vol 23, no 6 (1952)

Glubb, J.B. 'The Bedouins of Northern Iraq', *Journal of the Royal Central Asian Society*, vol **XXII**, Part 1 (1935)

Jarvis, Claude. *Yesterday and Today in Sinai* (London, 1931)

——'The Desert Bedouin and his Future', *Journal of the Royal Central Asian Society*, vol **XXIII**, Part 4 (1936)

——*Three Deserts* (London, 1936)

Jaussen, P. Antonin and Savignac. *Coutumes des Arabes au Pays de Moab* (Paris, 1908)

——*Coutumes des Fuqara* (Paris, 1914)

Katakura, Motoko. *Bedouin Village* (Tokyo, 1977)

——'Socioeconomic structure of a Bedouin settlement – a case study of Bushur, Saudi Arabia', *Bulletin of the Department of Geography* no 6 (University of Tokyo, 1974)

Lancaster, F. 'Bedouin by Adoption' *New Society* (31 January 1974)

Lancaster, W. 'I am your brother's son's son: help me', *New Society* (22 January, 1976)

Lawrence, T.E. *Seven Pillars of Wisdom* (London, 1935)

Montagne, R. *La Civilization du Desert: Nomades d'Orient et d'Afrique* (Paris, 1947)

Musil, Alois. *The Manners and Customs of the Rwala Bedouins* (New York, 1928)

Pritchard, E. Evans. *The Sanusi of Cyrenaica* (Oxford University Press, 1949)

Raswan, Carl. *The Black Tents of Arabia* (New York, 1947)

Thesiger, W. *Arabian Sands* (London, 1959)

Weir, Shelagh: *The Bedouin* (London, 1976) (Gives the most comprehensive bibliography of books and articles about the bedouin.)

Wellard, James. *The Great Sahara* (London, 1964)

ACKNOWLEDGEMENTS

The author and publishers wish to thank Cambridge University Press and Mrs A.A. Evans for permission to quote lines from Arberry, A.J., *Arabic Poetry,* and Dr William Polk for permission to quote from his translation of *The Golden Ode* by Labid Ibn Rabiah.

The author would also like to thank Mrs Violet Dickson, Mr William Lancaster, Dr Randall Baker, Mrs Motoko Katakura and Mr John Carter for the information which they so generously supplied.

INDEX

Numbers in italics indicate illustrations